CW00521159

UNCOMMON SENSE

Alternative Thinking on
Digital Transformation

Mark Aikman

Published by Toby Consulting Limited

For John, Christine and Steve, for starting the thinking

Acknowledgements

Grateful thanks to Mark Nicoll for insightful editing

CONTENTS

1. What are we doing here, then?

Introduction

> "Never doubt that a small group of thoughtful, committed citizens can change the world. Indeed, it's the only thing that ever has."
>
> ### *Margaret Mead*

Changing the world, eh? Your ambitions may be more along the lines of a more effective biscuit manufacturer than global transformation, but Mead's maxim still stands. With the right focus, a small insightful team can make it happen. This book gives some basic ideas on how to do that.

Like all management disciplines always seem to do, digital transformation has developed its very own sparkly circus of jargon, methodologies and smoke-and-mirrors special effects. The aim here is to offer a stimulating alternative perspective on digital change, because a dog-and-pony show is not really necessary. In reality, change is a common-sense activity; and this is a set of no-nonsense practical suggestions on how to achieve it.

There's no agreed definition of digital transformation: and you can't sit an exam on it. The term has been used to cover everything from just replacing paper to inventing Amazon. This book is simply my take on it. It's not a line-by-line guide – it's a resource to start you thinking.

What will this book cover? And ignore?

Perhaps best to begin with what this book is NOT. It's not a technical handbook or process roadmap. It's definitely not an academic textbook. It doesn't delve into the comparative merits of competing cloud solutions or give you a 1479-point checklist for installing a new ERP system – because hey, how dull would that be?

Instead, this is a book that sets out the key principles and techniques for leading a digital transformation, to get leaders started and ensuring they think as broadly as possible. It looks beyond the obvious (e.g. cloud solutions, ERP systems, dull stuff, etc), assuming the reader will have a grounding in the technical content of transformation. It doesn't cover stuff you can find in other generic management books – such as how to lead a team, benchmark effectively or run a project. It assumes you've got the ITIL Handbook and are not only using it to prop open your office door in warmer weather.

It doesn't claim to be a comprehensive guide leaving no stone unturned. Instead, it's a Thinking Starter Kit. It draws attention to the vast importance of people and their behaviour within change programmes, an aspect which can often be skimmed over. It looks at what it means day-to-day to lead a transformation programme. It takes an alternative view on relationships with colleagues, customers and suppliers.

On all these topics, it will introduce some ideas to consider and spark your thinking. And you, dear reader, will be perfectly able to take it from there.

Specifically, the book focuses on the parts of digital transformation that really make a programme a success, such as:

- Where to start
- Getting everyone to agree it's worth doing
- Ensuring the leadership team is onside
- Getting closer to the customers
- Persuading people in the organisation that they need to change
- Selecting and leading a successful team
- Keeping it – and you – safe
- Working to a deadline, a budget and great expectations
- Delivering at speed
- What to do if something goes wrong

Who might find it useful?

This is a book for people who are new to leading digital transformation programmes, or who are looking for fresh ideas or a couple of new approaches.

In addition, people in any role in organisations that are planning to undertake change might find it a thought-provoking read.

And it's a helicopter view of the subject for anyone who has oversight on a change programme – basically, The Cheats' Guide for CEOs.

How can you use it?

Read it all, or just dip in…

The chapters are arranged to cover chronologically what happens at each stage of a transformation (hey, it's not *that* alternative). At the end of many of them is a unique patent-pending copyright device, called *In Case of Emergency, Break Glass*. These sections include top tips on what to do to solve – or avoid - some classic transformation programme challenges.

And what the Sam Hill IS digital transformation?

Before we crack on, I think I need to explain what I mean by digital transformation. This is because I'm not convinced there is an agreed definition of what *everybody* means when they use this term. So, for me, it is:

Transformation: A posh word for change. I think that the old term, change, has no fundamental difference from "transformation", it's just a bit of jargon that's been adopted to make the process look shinier and brainier to outsiders.

For me, "change" has always meant "big change". So in this book, it will always mean "making things better for your business". It will mean genuine and often radical innovation, introducing something the organisation has never had before.

The change could be in the area of simplification, revenue generation, business model change: anything that fundamentally changes how things are done.

It's not about technical upgrades – it's about delivering your business in a new way. As an example: introducing new printers is not a digital transformation. But entirely removing printing from the organisation is.

The former is a technical upgrade – the latter is a whole new world of changed behaviour, risk and uncertainty!

Digital: "Digital" is ill-defined too. Basically, it means a change that involves new technology. But then, doesn't everything in life involve technology now?

So digital transformation will have new technology in it somewhere. But never assume that technology will always be primary the solution. Technology might be a possible solution you consider. It might be just the ticket. But sometimes, the solution might be the people or the process, instead. And as Transformation Lead, changing people and processes is your job, too.

2. Transformation v2.0

The demands of 2020s digital transformation

Within commercial businesses, IT is now in its forties, and looks like it's having a full-on red-sports-car-and-trendy-ankle-bashers mid-life crisis. I think I probably need to explain this before I can go on to look at the actions, responsibilities and necessary skills for digital transformation – because we need to view the Transformation Lead's role in context. I can then explain what demands are placed on the role and what needs to be different from the previous landscape. So….

The operating environment

IT overall is in a period of flux. As I see it, this has three key features that are relevant to digital transformation:

a) Skill shift

When I first started work, IT was quite clearly a business support function, there to speed up existing processes and save a few hours on record keeping and all that boring stuff. During my career, it's crept closer and closer to the heart of the business. By the Noughties, IT was getting asked what it thought about the Business Strategy, just to be sure we could make the plans work. But now, we're being asked to be thought-leaders in our businesses, being asked what we can suggest that'll help this business thrive, grow and anticipate/outstrip the competition.

Therefore, we are being asked to develop new skillsets – from understanding strategy and marketing to thinking creatively and commercially. And this is needed alongside all the skills we previously needed, like having time to mend the server and order the ink for the printers. We are now expected to keep an eye on looking after the back-room-big-stuff, whilst paying full attention to the here-and-now-and-tomorrow-too.

Therefore, my first point is, embrace your role in leading and developing your organisation. It might not be what you were originally trained for, but it's definitely a contribution you can make. When the going gets tough – and it will – don't revert to the safe old world of technology and technicality, but instead keep a focus on building this business.

b) *Our old five-speed gearbox might not now be fast enough*

The hippy child of the seventies, IT spent a lot of the 90s becoming "safe". We invented protocols and best practice and procedures and guidelines and all that ITIL stuff. This allowed IT-uninitiated colleagues to trust us to get on with our bit of the business without bankrupting them or designing the IT equivalent of Mousetrap. It made us more careful and reliable, but slower.

As the demand for market-responsiveness picks up, we probably cannot continue to be as slow and steady. We need to be prepared to jump-to-it when our colleagues in marketing demand customer-driven augmented-reality innovations, for next Tuesday. We will all need to move towards agile and continuous improvement of IT, maybe never arriving at the final finishing line. We may even have to consider whether PRINCE 2 should go the same way as The Artist Formerly Known As...

c) There is less emphasis on technological knowledge

In the last 20 years, we've driven Clarkson-like through centralised mainframe batch driven processing; to the client server; then to individual data centres; then up, up and away into the cloud. We've gone from five-and-a-quarter-inch floppies, to 3.5 inch stiffies, with a significant amount of the budget spent on data storage. Now, we have WAY too much data – big or otherwise – and so much of it that we now need data science to find it: and it's all being stored for 20p!

Now, we may have to shift our focus from data *storage* to marshalling that data; being able to interpret it; and make it useful to the business. We may not even need to know about data technology. After all, we won't be buying it, or housing it; just renting it as a service and letting it run happily in the ether, with someone else providing all the maintenance and R&D.

This is an example of how we are becoming translators of technology for other parts of the business: you know, like helping marketing make best use of virtual reality for an authentic customer experience….

Back in the day, the IT Director was the uber-techie, the guy who'd learned about Unix, Pascal and C++ and could fit the green-and-white striped paper into the dot matrix printer. He (and I mean "he" 98% of the time) was there to answer the questions of the more junior techie-trained team. He listened politely if ever called into the Executive Team meeting, where they told him what they wanted, then went away and made it happen. Across the forty years, he (and a few shes), have had a hard fight for a place at that boardroom table.

So now, the IT Lead may need to be much less technologically aware. There is probably a greater role for an IT leader to be a change manager, a marketing partner and an empowering motivator of other people across the organisation.

Transformation v2.0

Just as IT overall is moving into v2.0, I believe IT transformation programmes are entering their second generation. In future, most transformation focus will not be on the mega-moves, with giant infrastructure replacements taking years, but with – eventually - an end date. Instead, transformation will largely become continuous flux, constantly updating to outpace the market – perpetual evolution, not one-off revolution.

Therefore, in this context, I'd argue that the digital transformation lead plays the following role; experiences significant pressures and demands; and needs specific skills and qualities:

1. No more Mr Nice Guy

V1.0 Heads of IT Transformation politely fulfilled the company's expectations, on request. In future, there'll be no more Mr Nice Guy. From now on, you may find yourself in the uncomfortable position of pointing out that the Emperor isn't wearing any clothes. Instead of doing as you're told, you could well be coming into the boardroom with tales of doom, pointing out that our business could halve overnight if our sector's equivalent of Amazon or Uber is gearing up out there…..

In future, you may be in the position where they call you the CIO but they think it stands for Change and Impermanence Officer – you'll be the person who is reviled for never letting people settle into a comfortable routine, always demanding they are agile and open to new ways of doing things.

The transformational lead will need the confidence, tenacity and energy to continue to live like this and keep on driving the programme.

2. A new place on the grid

Traditionally, IT came under the wing of Finance, or sat quietly beside the COO. For continuous transformation, you're going to need some new friends.

First, you'll need to sit closely with the customers. Their expectations, often driven by their experiences as consumers, will evolve rapidly and you'll need to be alert to what they need and want.

In turn, that means you'll need to get closer to sales and marketing. This is happening quite organically in many organisations as IT and Marketing partner on digital marketing initiatives. But it needs to be closer still. Like, daily.

And because your work will throw all the company's employees into a permanent Discomfort Zone, you'll need a stronger working relationship with HR. You'll need to get very good at the people-stuff: more follows….

3. *Out there*

In future, you will need to get out there. No more sitting high in the ivory tower and directing operations. You will need an excellent understanding of how people in this business actually do things. You'll also need to know what will motivate them to change; what will smooth their transition to new ways of working; and what changes they suggest themselves.

You need all this information because you'll be very closely involved in getting the IT changes implemented, adopted and loved. That means you'll be contributing ideas to objectives, rewards and "openness to change" training. You'll need to be involved in things that never previously looked like IT, like getting everyone on the bus. Oh, that's right – a true partner in the business…

4. The cultural architect

Culture matters. You will not deliver if you don't address culture. That's why old-school take-the-money-and-run off-the-shelf delivery by consultants and external suppliers always needs to be customised later – because it didn't quite suit us.

It's your job to create the culture for change. Your solution has to fit the real world of your organisation, but be motivating enough for people to want to make the effort to change. So save time – build the culture into the solution from the start. Be a listener who takes time to truly understand As Is. Be an inspiring influencer who sells the need for the change to everyone from the Chair to the Char. Hire the right people for the Programme who will be passionate ambassadors for change. Yes, you are the Champion Cheerleader for Change.

5. An agile mindset

No, I'm not using agile in the sense of agile development. I'm talking bigger than that. I would define the agile mindset that Transformation Leads need as one that has no fear of innovation – even on a large scale, with risk and/or at high speed. It is a mindset confident to make changes because the basis for the change is rooted in intelligent analysis and well-considered weighing of alternative solutions. And the agile mindset means you are able to take decisions on innovation quickly because you have had your eye on the wider horizon in the preceding months and years. You saw this coming.

6. *Even more Mr Nice Guy*

And finally, a clarification. Our organisations at first might see us and our agile change initiatives as "no more Mr Nice Guy" – but in fact, we'll need to be EVEN more Mr Nice Guy.

We all know that people don't like change. And that's not just dyed-in-the-wool lifers who have been here since the organisation was three people and a hut. It's people with a natural disposition to dislike rapid/continuous change. These people occupy all roles and ranks in a business.

So on a personal level, you'll need a superlative set of people-skills – empathy, persuasion, influencing, engagement skills, charm... and the best communication skills in the business.

3. T-Time

How to tell if you need digital transformation

People working in IT can get hung up on the "evolution or revolution" debate. When does your IT just need a bit of tweaking; and when do you need full-throttle IT transformation? For me, it doesn't really matter – it's academic, and not worth devoting too much headspace to. I don't think it's necessary to decide which kind, because you will probably be overtaken by external events anyway, as you progress.

However, you DO need to be able to recognise when it's time for you to take some kind of action. I believe there are five symptoms that show an organisation is in need of something approaching the full monty. This questionnaire walks you through them:

1)   Is your screen still black and green?

If it is, you're using some 30-plus-year-old technology that hasn't yet made it into the digital age, and it's time to bite the transformation bullet. And bear in mind, black-and-green is indicative of Big-Hair 80s technology in its underwear. We are talking COBOL, DB2, C and (worst case) Assembly Language, that kind of gig. There are plenty of those systems dressed up in a party frock, with modern-looking interface screens but that are still really black and green underneath....

2) Is your Head of IT ranked below C-Suite level?

If he/she is, then this person – and this discipline - is not considered to be integral to the business. He/she is not in a position to influence strategic decisions. IT is therefore still being seen as a tool, not an integrated leader or enabler. Those days are over.

As the IT lead, you can prove IT's worth to the business by the act of transforming. As the business comes to realise what IT can do for it – and where it can take the organisation – your worth will become immediately apparent.

3) Does your technology dictate unsuitable processes?

You know the sort of thing: Barry gets the figures off the system and exports them to a spreadsheet. He then passes that spreadsheet on to Graham, who cross-references it with *his* spreadsheet. Then Graham sends it to Janice who adds it up and writes a paragraph to go with it. And bingo! The answer you need in just three hours and 16 easy stages! Bad technology does nothing other than teach your team how to invest their time in developing ingenious local solutions….

4) Is technology is excluded from your R&D programme?

If you're developing products and services without thinking about the technology content, then you're a taxi firm that's waiting to be overtaken by Uber. You need technology to help you to be disruptive in your sector, to innovate and to get the edge. You need it built in to your offer, not added on at the end – or you're at risk of being overtaken by an app developed in a back-bedroom.

5) Is your IT department still kept in cupboard?

Stand-alone IT departments are looking increasingly lonely. In these, techies sit in their quiet office waiting to be invited out for a day out in the rest of the company; or retreat there to escape the ear-bashing from irate colleagues who don't know how to explain what the problem is. Instead, embedding IT people into the other disciplines (e.g. Marketing, Finance, Production) has been proven to enable greater productivity. The host disciplines have less downtime; their systems become sleeker and faster with a techie on the ground; and the Hero Techie spots and stops a disaster *before* it happens.

So in the time-honoured style of glossy magazine quizzes: if you have answered "yes" to two or more of the above questions, then you need to read on…

4. See it, sell it, solve it

The principles of transformation

Digital transformation can be extremely intimidating. Believe me, even when you've spent your entire career in transformation, it still looks like a cliff viewed from the beach on your first day at work.

Therefore, as a framework for thinking about your transformation, it may be helpful if I set out some first principles. I think there are nine golden rules (because ten would be corny).

1) Set a vision that everyone can believe in

Bottom line 1: there's no success without vision. But large bespoke digital transformations can take a long time and are incredibly complex. They contain an infinite number of opportunities to become side-tracked. They can be hijacked by ever-changing technologies; they are often subject to organisational regime changes; and they serve colleagues with widely differing priorities.

I've learned that it's critical to solidify the vision of what the programme will enable the organisation to do – and to do this very quickly. It's then essential to create a simple message about the vision that people can remember; and which makes the benefits of the programme crystal clear. Typically, the vision should state what the transformation will help the business achieve.

Then, everyone working on the programme will have an easy-to-remember yardstick that will help them decide on whether something is a necessity or a priority, instead of just a nice-to-have.

The vision is a magical management tool because it empowers the team to deliver. When you have intelligent and capable people who understand and rate the vision, they do not need anyone to tell them every day precisely what to do. Many will immediately take the initiative and bring forward great ideas, all on-message; others will learn how to have confidence and the courage of their convictions. These people will feel that they are making a contribution and that they have opportunities for creativity and autonomy. They experience the satisfaction of being both permitted and encouraged to think for themselves.

Therefore, communicating a clear vision and understanding of the benefits of the programme will encourage better and quicker decision making; reduce wasted effort; and create an energetic and engaged delivery team. That's where productivity lies.

But the vision is not just a framework for the transformation team. It's a tool to win over the whole organisation. You will need to communicate the vision as widely as possible. Your aim should be to persuade people throughout the organisation that it's useful, an improvement, worth the effort, and even downright sexy. You need company-wide buy-in.

Once your vision is set, your job is then to be the keeper of the vision, challenging any flights of fancy that fall outside the central requirement.

2) Put the customer front and centre

In all transformations, the customer must be the central point of focus. "Customers" are easy to identify in commercial businesses (they buy things, see). Their role is played by "service users" in non-commercial organisations. Common sense.

In digital transformation, customer-centric perspective has to be coupled with a rapid response to that customer's ever-changing needs. And those needs do change quickly – for example, nobody knew they needed an app to call a cab instead of making a phone call, until Uber showed them how handy one could be. Or no-one thought more than half of UK pensioners would take up online shopping in two months in 2020, until Covid hit. Customers are often keener than we think to change the way they interact with a brand.

We need accurate information, constantly updated, on what the customers are thinking. And the transformation activity needs to be buzzing around these views and needs, working very quickly and nimbly.

The customer is always moving. Customers' expectations will change, as will their appetite for new and niftier solutions.

Alongside this, we need to be observing the actions of competitors, not just leaving that to Marketing or Sales.

This is not something that only Marketing should monitor. The Transformation Lead needs an open mind and a keen eye on how customers are behaving. But developing access to customer information and observation needs to be in collaboration with the traditional customer-facing functions. Therefore, I strongly recommend you *befriend* your internal information gatherers rather than muscling-in, treading on toes or knowing better.

3)   Engage everyone

Face outwards
The transformation team needs to face outwards. For too long, IT teams have lived in a world where they are expected to be head down, keeping the machinery running, while the big decisions were taken by other people. That era is over. We can no longer operate by considering only our own teams or organisations – meerkat-like, we need to sit up and look around.

Listen to the C-suite
Early on, you will need to engage with the organisation's leadership team. That means time spent on listening, observing and taking the time to truly understand the ideas and concerns of C-Suite colleagues   You will then have the fuller picture and be in a position to respond nimbly.

Make time to persuade

After that, it will be necessary to persuade. We have all noticed over the years that people within the organisation tend not to do things simply because we tell them to. Instead, they have to be persuaded. Therefore, I'm saying that a key mindset *and skillset* for Transformation Lead is the ability to persuade, influence and communicate. You will need to prove the argument for your innovation logically and with evidence, as has always been case. But you will also need to be able to influence C-Suite colleagues with persuasive arguments, as well as having the background-radiation of credibility as an outward looking, market-responsive thinker.

Next, you will need to make the case for change to everyone else in the organisation - the people whose roles and processes will change. That will need to be framed to include:

- logical arguments for the changes
- understanding the benefits to those affected
- communicating results to the business and its teams

Only with all three strands in place can you even hope that people will sample and then adopt the changes.

Crucially, the Transformation Lead needs to understand that the endless chatter that underpins persuading and influencing is in fact, Real Work. And it is activity that will consume a great deal of their working week. Talking is a Proper Job.

Everyone on the bus

As I said above, we need everyone buying-into the vision. But we can't just wash our hands of them once they have an understanding of the vision: we have to bring them along through the whole experience too. As everyone knows, significant change of any kind can be a challenging and often even a threatening experience. And most people don't react well to being threatened!

We have to have everyone firmly on the bus to achieve programme success.

In a digital transformation, there is a very important virtuous circle that can oh-so easily become a vicious circle. It's the relationship between digital change and cultural change. Digital change absolutely inevitably forces cultural and behavioural change on the organisation's people – things are just plain done differently. But equally, cultural change will be needed if the digitisation is to become wholeheartedly adopted.

So we need continuous work to keep all those people keen on the digital improvements we're making. That means every programme needs massive effort directed towards building and maintaining workforce engagement. Which means...

Communication is more important than technology

The technology choices we make pale into insignificance behind the communication choices. The most technologically-brilliant solution has no credence whatsoever if you haven't got the communication piece right. So business and stakeholder engagement – getting people onside and keeping them there – will be pivotal to the success of your project.

Your communication needs to be empathetic, standing in the shoes of your listeners. My favourite example of this is from a major change programme we delivered for a traditional business, which included a great deal of technology to speed up processes. Such technology always has the potential to threaten people – faster processes translate quickly to mean fewer jobs, for a suspicious workforce. But our CEO took the decision early to expressly state that improved processes would not mean job losses. All time gained would be invested in further developing customer care – not in the dreaded efficiency savings – because that was what was right for this brand and this business. This helped people immediately view the programme as a positive benefit to their working lives, and not a threat. Engagement was on a firm footing.

You may not be in a position to promise that: but there will always be another attractive benefit you can hang your hat on.

4) Quick response is always possible

When a global pandemic hit in 2020, we all proved that a quick response is possible. Well, we had no choice but to change at high speed if our organisations were to continue to exist. I'd argue that it's *always* possible to respond quickly, and that availability of choice has nothing to do with it.

The most pressured transformation I have ever undertaken was when I led deployment on the fastest and largest ever separation in the food industry. I helped set up the world's largest plant-based food manufacturer (makers of Flora, I Can't Believe It's Not Butter) as the firm separated from global giant Unilever. We had to achieve the transformation within 22 months, configuring and installing a new ERP system, across 14 manufacturing plants and lord-knows-how-many offices on all continents, in three phases. "Quick" doesn't even begin to do it justice.

But we made it, and that was due to (hard work and) taking one significant decision: to use out-of-the-box solutions, with little to no customisation, adaptation or personalisation. Instead, we changed the old organisation's processes to adapt to the customers' requirements and the technology solutions. That enabled rapid and customer-focused change to occur. The new organisation's processes simply followed where the IT led.

So, if speed is what matters most, it can be done. If you are up against a very tight deadline, non-customised solutions will get you there: and certainly, that's reasonably easy to achieve when you are setting up a new organisation. It's also a possible solution when there is significant, rapid and/or permanent market change, i.e. when the organisation is in survival mode. Frankly, when it's change or die – the people and processes tend to run with whatever the technology imposes.

If you're in a situation where it's essential you bring hearts and minds along with you, it's still perfectly possible to achieve rapid change. For this, you need a two-pronged approach – some form of agile development: and heavy emphasis on persuasion and communication. Agile development allows you to change one-piece-at-a-time and is often a good way to win people over: for example, quickly changing a clunky time-consuming process will often gain supporters for the programme in its early stages.

To keep going with an agile development schedule, though, you will need a heavyweight communication campaign to persuade all users that continuous change is worth the disruption.

5) Do your Discovery first

It's amazing how many transformation programmes start by looking for the technology solution – without first identifying how the organisation needs to change.

So instead of solution-ising to prove how clever and knowledgeable you are, listen first to people from across the business. What do they want and need? That touch of humility will go a long way towards beginning the engagement between your programme and this business.

6) Choose technologies that truly benefit the business

Successful innovation isn't always about the bleeding-edge. Of course, everyone wants to out-run obsolescence but it's essential not to be diverted by hot-off-the-press technologies and solutions. They're sexy, sure – but are they what this business really needs?

I learned early that the newest solution isn't by definition the best. Instead, it's essential to balance the technology specification, design and build against those business benefits we truly need. So if the business needs bells but not whistles, take care not to get distracted by using whistles, just because they're there and they're noisy.

Innovative technology can appear particularly attractive when an organisation is replacing something antique. In that situation, people can be so exasperated by elderly technology that they focus excitedly on the bright lights of the very latest and trendiest technology.

The rule for selecting technology should be: does it benefit the customer? If it doesn't benefit the customer directly, does it help the smooth running of the business (which in turn will benefit the customer in the long run)? And those benefits might be "soft" and intangible, as well as ROI-based. So, for example, if an item of technology speeds up a process, that's great, we can use it: because the time saved on running that process can then be invested in further developing customer care.

The question "what's right for this business?" is invaluable in helping you select a suite of technologies that perfectly fit your needs. Technology selections need to be unbiassed. At the outset, aim to avoid leaning towards particular solutions that some commentators feel should be used. Use nothing that's there for the sake of it; and don't buy over-stuffed packages or over-complex systems.

I'm intrigued by just how long it's taking our sector to adopt the latest technologies. Where is the real-world, fully-implemented, AI, machine learning, robotics, blockchain and all that jazz? Why are we not climbing over each other to be first to market with it? Maybe it's this kind of pragmatism – or maybe it's fear. It could be that the technologies are there but Transformation Leads and organisations just don't know quite what the customer benefit this new technology truly represents.

Or it could be that we DO know precisely how new technology could benefit the organisation and its customers. However, we are surrounded by people who are afraid that leaping into the unknown and using unproven technology might be too risky. The CFO worries about cost; the CMO worries about reputational risk; the CTO worries that the technology we're looking at might be superseded by next Tuesday; and the CEO just sees TSB and Travelex and worries... So we're having to model, pilot, test, retest, remodel the retest, and test the pilot (twice; once in a sealed room)... and so none of us are anywhere near going live. Safe to say, there's no shame in avoiding cutting-edge innovation if you don't absolutely need it.

Oh, and finally: sometimes, technology isn't the answer at all! Just because this is a digital transformation, not everything needs to be solved digitally.

7) Strong relationships matter

Rule 7 seems obvious: relationships matter. We all understand that in close-up – such as our relationships with those we work with every day. But it is also extremely important to recognise the importance of productive relationships with those more-occasional participants in the programme – such as the minor suppliers; the Board; light-users of the system; or Programme auditors.

Without positive relationships with these less-obvious stakeholders, the programme will fail at one hurdle or another. So that key question above has a slight extension: what's right for **everyone in and around** this business?

8) Keep the objective in focus

Let me tell you a story from long, long ago:

Once upon a time, my team had been called in because a project had stalled. The aim was to migrate thousands of mailboxes from internal hosting on one platform to external hosting on another, in a multi-national company. The budget was £9m. In a year, £5m had been spent: and 160 people were working on it.

And not one single mailbox had gone anywhere at all.

Yes, it was complicated – these mailboxes were in a variety of countries; some were shared; they were all huge; users would need re-training; it was political; the supplier was tough; blah, blah, blah – you'll have heard it all before.

But to me, that was no excuse for why nothing had actually happened and precisely nothing had been achieved. Those involved were busy considering all the possibilities and eventualities, in theory. They'd perfected a number of nice-to-haves, like training and technology comparisons. They'd done a lot of things would eventually need doing – but mainly, they'd done stuff that didn't need doing YET. And indeed, most of them hadn't even met each other – they were all working hard, in blinkers-on mode, on their own little bit.

What was needed was a back-to-basics approach. We needed to migrate a mailbox or two. Because, after all, this programme was all about moving mailboxes.

This way, we could put the programme back in the real world – doing what it says on the tin. So we migrated some mailboxes to the new platform/host. We migrated a few complicated and jumbo-sized ones. Internationally. Overnight. Doing logistical back-flips. It was extremely simple – we just **tested** the idea.

And we observed and measured what happened. That allowed us to refine our processes and ideas, improve them, and start developing a model based in reality. We were back in the real world. So we moved some more, observed, measured, refined our plans....

The lesson I took from this is that it is essential to keep in mind just one question: "What are we trying to achieve with this programme?"

This question is absolutely crucial to the success of all programmes and needs to be asked... every day. Some key principles to ensure that you stick to delivering the objective are:

Just do it: In digital transformation, you CANNOT have it all ironed out in theory before you start. You can't plan for perfection because life – and IT, and people – doesn't allow for that. So keep it real and go for the Do-Measure-Improve model: try a step of what you want to do; observe how it goes: and then work out how you can get better and better at it. Don't go too early to the stuff we don't need to think about just yet – chances are, the goalposts will have moved by the time we get there.

You'll make most progress towards the objective when you're moving, not thinking.

Keep the objective front of everyone's mind: Never lose sight of what the programme is all about – and ensure the whole team thinks the same way. Ask someone every day: "tell me what we want to be able to do here." By getting a simple answer to this simple question, you identify and reinforce the core focus of the programme. You – and your colleagues - know what the key activities and content have to be. You therefore also will always know what's real and what is just white noise. People are unlikely to wander too far down side-alleys.

There still has to be a plan: The programme nonetheless has to have a structure.   Every sub-team has to know what they're here to do; and with whose work their own needs to interlock. Everyone needs roles and responsibilities, all of which fit together jigsaw-like. That's the only theory you concern yourself with before you start Doing Stuff. But don't get too hung up on *precisely* what they're all going to do, setting it in stone on Day 1.

Bear in mind that it's highly likely that Do-Measure-Improve will send you down many unexpected paths. You therefore need people to be nimble and relaxed about what needs to be done; and who's doing what. Transformation is no place for the fixated.

There's only one programme: Clearly, I'm shouting loudly about getting the whole business enthused and involved in your transformation. We want people to want it. If people want to contribute, that's absolutely marvellous.

But this strategy has one minor drawback – enthusiastic, well-intentioned side-alleys.

People who passionately want the organisation to change and/or those who don't think your Programme is moving quickly enough for their liking will want to contribute their own changes. Even though I'm a firm believer in many hands making light work, sub-projects that don't fall within your governance can be damaging. There's a risk that these projects will include contradictory processes or incompatible technologies.

Therefore, your strategy has to be to get all the enthusiasts inside your tent. By all means they can run sub-teams and working parties, but with all projects scrutinised and approved by the central Programme Office before progression.

And yes, that means winning their collaboration early doors.

Anything might happen (but it probably won't): Don't get carried away feeling you must anticipate every possibility. Living through a pandemic can get you like that.

Yes, in transformation you do need to abide by the principle that anything might happen. However, I advise against setting up A War-Room of Possibilities. Instead, you will need a rolling headline plan for what we will do if outlying situations occur, but you should primarily concentrate on having responses up your sleeve for the more *likely* probabilities. We need one foot in the future – but the likely future.

And of course, you will need, as ever, to keep abreast of technology innovations. However, don't reduce the role into becoming the Librarian of New Advances. Primarily, focus on selecting customer-responsive business innovations and *then* cherry-pick the right kit to deliver the objective.

9) Deliver

If the first bottom line is to set a vision; then the second bottom line is to deliver. There's no success without delivery. In full, in budget, on time. Also, there's no credibility without delivery, so you need to deliver if you are to keep the organisation on-side.

The programme needs to be seen to be delivering against pre-agreed outcomes/results/milestones. This is where governance really matters. It is essential to agree the requirements and then check-in with the programme sponsors very regularly, to demonstrate requirements are being/will be delivered. Yes, slippage happens. In fact, it almost always happens. But as long as delivery remains your focus as Transformation Lead, and that the sponsors are aware of the effect of changing requirements on your ability to deliver, you can always get it out of the door by a deadline that meets with their approval.

5. Ideas, innovation and influence

Leadership of digital transformation

Now then, leadership. No, hang on, wait, just a minute! Please don't skip to the next chapter. I am quite sure you know all about leading a team – and I'm with Terry Leahy's ten words on this, my three favourites being truth, trust and simplicity – so I won't waste your time with that. Instead, this is about leadership specific to a transformation programme.

Leadership of digital transformation operates two pairs of principles:

- Ideas and innovation: be outward looking and inventive; and anticipate the future rather than reflect the present.
- Influence: win hearts and minds; and keep these tied to you with a red silk ribbon.

First, some ideas on business innovation within your Programme:

Thinking big

As Head of Transformation, you have an enormous responsibility for thought-leadership. You're here to run the show and deliver, couldn't agree more, but it's also your responsibility to make the Programme as innovative as it can possibly be, within your stated purpose.

As Programme Thought Leader, you're looking for ideas that think big that you can explore. What can you include that will actually *change the business* and not just improve operational effectiveness? The latter is a given in transformation – the former is what will add true benefit.

So don't be too quick to dismiss seemingly disruptive or over-ambitious ideas – there may be a genuine benefit to the business in what is being described, even though it currently sounds a bit sci-fi. Especially at the early doors stage, keep away from language that dismisses the more revolutionary ideas until you've investigated the benefit vs. achievability ratio. So we're not saying "Utopia", "pipe-dream", "fantasyland" or even "unrealistic". And we're definitely never saying "crackpot".

One important point on this: thought-leadership does **not** mean "I *personally* must have all the good ideas". Indeed, implementing only your own (crackpot) ideas is counter-productive as it will quickly reduce team buy-in.

Instead, the thought leader is there to raise the bar and widen the horizons, so that your team and your colleagues in the wider business can have the innovative ideas. Effectively, you are the ideas-coach. Allow multiple opportunities for creative solution development – from capturing innovations at the Discovery stage; the workshopping possible options; to championing inventive routes to market suggested by junior people. And let all the original thinkers have their moment in the sun.

Looking Forward

You can make an excellent return on the investment in your Programme if it includes a degree of future-proofing. Again, you need to work entirely within your stated objectives, but you should always consciously focus on anticipating what's coming next.

One of the biggest enemies of anticipation is thin Discovery. Programmes which have selected the technology solution before understanding the problems and opportunities (i.e. a good majority of them) will not hear the still small voices that have seen the future. These Programmes have wedged themselves into the here and now, using technology that's already available to address issues that exist today.

At least give a few days' thought to where your organisation and sector will go tomorrow. Rope-in Marketing and ask them what their opium-crazed predictions include as possibilities for your field. It won't all be spaceships and fantasy and they'll have evidence for the most likely scenarios.

However far behind your systems are, your aim is never catching up with The Now.

The second aspect of leadership in digital transformation is your role in influencing – you are the last layer of Araldite that sticks the business to the Programme.

Dobbin, you're looking a bit thirsty, lad!

Taking horses to water is the easy bit, so I'm told. I assume when they get there, they just stand around, looking a tad sceptical. This scenario regularly plays out in transformation.

I'm talking about the burning need for more than just superficial buy-in to your Programme. Programmes fall down when they only have token engagement from a business that is simply standing next to the trough.

Now, I'm not suggesting that you need to get the entire organisation ragingly passionate about your transformation and, ahem, lapping it up. That would be nice, but in the real world, you'll be doing very well indeed if you have pockets of passionate engagement, with the rest of the organisation reaching lukewarm or just neutral.

So, token engagement occurs when you've set out your vision and communicated your objectives and blueprint (Chapter 7): and no-one has told you to stop what you're doing. This situation exemplifies an organisation which has been taken to water. You have not got it to drink. Yet it is very common for Programme Leads to believe that by announcing the plan, with no arguments, they've arrived at support and acceptance.

No. It's now Forth-Bridge time. You now need to begin a Programme-long campaign of appetite-generation. You need a vast campaign of enthusiasm-generating engagement, and so I make no apologies for droning on endlessly about the principles and techniques of this throughout this book.

Keeping the dressing room onside

Having won your friends (or at least, made very few enemies), now you need to keep them onside.

Team sponsor

Every Programme must have an Executive Sponsor. This is always a senior person – ideally your CEO or equivalent, but definitely a C-Suiter – who has two seemingly-paradoxical roles: fan club and referee.

The Executive Sponsor's first role is to champion the Programme with senior stakeholders in your organisation – your cheer-leading fan-club. This person will hold a position which has more assumed influence (i.e. power) than you have. This person will communicate the importance and indispensability of your Programme; be your eyes, ears and mouth for conversations at the most senior level; and front-up against resistance on your behalf, if necessary. That's his/her public role.

In private, (s)he's your referee, calling you out for handballs, offsides and dodgy tackles. Governance activities all report to your Sponsor. This person has to have full trust that you will lead your team to deliver and will not embarrass him/her, having been given the support described above.

Consequently, your Sponsor is the most important person to keep onside. We all know how "having the full confidence of the Chairman" translates, and we don't want to get anywhere near that point.

You will keep this trust very simply, with two techniques:

- **Deliver**. Demonstrating progress within the agreed parameters will allow your Sponsor to defend you at every turn: and

- **Be honest**. If it's not working; or you are not going to make the deadline/budget/expectations, you need to honestly admit to it. More below.

Team effort

I also want to make the point that, again, you are not alone when it comes to getting the crowd behind you. Engagement is a dispersed responsibility, which has two key types of players:

- **Your executive sponsor:** Your champion within the C-suite must understand that his/her role is to schmooze and dazzle all those who are at below-neutral levels of support. Honest but unfailing support – at least in public – for the Programme is this person's responsibility. So don't team up with a sponsor who can't commit to this. Politicians need not apply.

- **The entire transformation team:** Change managers aren't the only people responsible for change happening. Communications people aren't the only spreaders of the word. Trainers aren't the only educators. These responsibilities are shouldered by the whole transformation team – no footballing analogy necessary. As Head of Programme, a key leadership task is that you give your team the skills to enthuse the wider organisation about the Programme and its benefits. They are all ambassadors, whose daily responsibility is to recruit and inspire more ambassadors.

Accept the yellow cards

As I touched on above, honesty is the best policy. That's because you have to be honest to be trusted – not just by your sponsor, but by everyone leading or working in the organisation.

Therefore, maintaining trust and engagement means accepting the yellow cards without argument. Just as it does on the pitch, early acceptance of a mistake or problem ensures the incident blows over quickly and there's no need for the referee to start reaching for the red card. Two situations in which it's good leadership to be honest at top speed are:

- Any point at which you know you can't deliver as planned, whether that's the deadline or the chosen technology. Admit it's not working and propose a Plan B. Your Governance structures (Chapter 9) give you a space in which to do this without a big drama.

  Don't hang on, hoping it might get better; the developers might suddenly become efficient; or the price might miraculously go down. Fess up, cut your losses and crack on.

- Any point at which you know you're not the right person for the job. If you cannot continue with a Programme you no longer believe in, then put yourself on the transfer list. You will doubtlessly go on to have far more success at Oldham Athletic.

Work with the Line Judge

Finally, one tip on balancing two roles of programme leadership – keeping the business enthusiastic and engaged: and saying no.

You will regularly find yourself in the difficult position of needing to keep a colleague committed to the transformation but not being able to accommodate a particular feature in the Programme.

The indispensable referee's assistant here is your Head of Security. Think nightclub.

Over the last decade, CISOs have come to the fore, as the importance of security is recognised. They are there to keep the organisation safe.

In the same period, responsibility for technology has become more widely dispersed across the business – for example, Marketing may have chosen the CRM system; or Finance may have oversight on the accounting tools used. Therefore, there are local "Centres of Excellence" at best, and "territories" at worst, throughout many organisations.

So if your Centres of Excellence are looking for tools that are, after much soul-searching, truly incompatible with your bigger Programme, you will sadly have to say no. This has the potential to do significant damage to levels of engagement from those quarters.

However; it is almost always the case that incompatibility equals security risk. And everyone in Marketing knows the damage a security breach will do to the brand. Just like everyone in Finance knows what damage a security breach would do to the bank account. So make sure you have your biggest bouncer standing behind you, hands loosely clasped at waist height, when you break the news….

In case of emergency, break glass

Losing the sponsor

It's tough at the top, so I've heard. It's particularly tough being an executive sponsor, walking the narrow path between Programme Promoter and Programme Police Officer.

When the chips are down, it can be quite easy for an inexperienced Programme Sponsor to take sides. If she is siding with you and your Programme, and is furious with the rest of the organisation, stop reading this paragraph and go straight to *Failure to Engage*, below. But if she's jumped the other way, and is ganging up with the C-Suite to hold your feet to the fire, here are some points to think carefully about:

- What concerns is she stating? Are these limited to a particular feature, area or problem within the Programme, or are they widespread and diverse?
- Are her concerns due to lack of understanding or reassurance? Or are they in fact well-founded concerns? Be honest here. With yourself.
- Has something changed in her world during the course of the Programme, such as the arrival of a new CEO who is less enamoured of what we're doing than the previous incumbent?

- Is she giving "good reasons" for her discomfort, or "real reasons"? For example, a "good reason" might be the claim that Supplier A is proving expensive; but the "real reason" is that the CEO took a dislike to Supplier A and she needs to regain the CEO's respect.
- Do you have any reason to believe she may be experiencing Programme Fatigue – over-work, other significant demands on her attention, boredom, frustration, or exasperation at the rate of change?

You may or may not be able to answer these questions and have confidence that your assessment is correct. If you're not sure of the answers to any of them – *and* to check out your assumptions even if you think you've got a handle on the situation – there's only one thing for it….

Ask her. Talk it through.

This is not a confrontation. It's a low-key, honest conversation in which you ask her what her concerns are and leave non-defensive silence and space for her answers. And take it from there.

6. Silence please, communication

in progress

Discovery

Discovery is what you do first. That might not stack up with what I said in "T-Time" (Chapter 3), when I was banging on about the clues that tell you what you need to transform. I might have misled you into the impression that you need to crack-on with replacing your COBOL system and that's all you need to know.

No. You may have spotted your Big Issue (green and black screens dating from the heyday of Duran Duran), but you're nowhere near out of the starting blocks. You have an awareness of a core technology problem, but at this stage you now desperately need to know about Es - Everything Else.

To do that, you will need to listen and observe. To Olympic standard.

What do you need to achieve from the discovery phase?

Discovery works on more levels than simply finding out how people currently use the existing technology. It has six key features:

1. What's going on in this organisation?

Simple. Discovery tells you what's going on in the organisation. Who's doing what with which technology; whether it works or not; how they cheat when it doesn't work; how we could do more business if it worked differently; and how it could be brillianter. It creates benchmark baselines of where we are now on your chosen yardsticks – such as how long it currently takes to do stuff.

You need to elicit a comprehensive picture of what will make the business more efficient and effective, and ideally future-proofed.

Of course, this opens us up to kite-flying pipe-dreams and Utopian-Nirvanas of the first water. It can be very easy for Discovery to conclude that Everything Is Broke and Only Perfection Will Do as a solution. But that's OK as a starting point: you are aiming to get a sense of the biggest picture possible. Managing expectations comes later. A full sense of what's wrong and what's an opportunity will help you scope the project and prioritise its component parts.

2. What's the people-factor?

You will also need an understanding of the people of the organisation – widely termed the culture, but exemplified by attitudes and behaviour they demonstrate. You'll need to get a clear picture of which frustrations are so great that they outweigh resistance to change – this is generally expressed as "*anything* would be better than this"!

You'll need to know who is supporting which agenda, from the C-suite right through to the shop-floor. You'll need an attitudinal map, understanding, for example, which departments are the most crafty work-arounders; which will be impressed by glitzy gizmos and gorgeous gadgets; and which would prefer Slade to still be topping the charts.

3. What about the customers?

Let's have a little story, seeing life from the customer's end of the telescope….

Stuck on an extremely stationary train once, short of entertainment, my colleague and I were having a conversation – well, OK, a two-way rant – about the transport and travel industry. We concluded that clearly, ten years ago, some imaginative IT and/or Marketing people in travel were given a problem statement that asked them to address "profitable, customer-focused booking". Some of them did an absolutely brilliant job: for example, just look at the intuitive and innovative approaches in the Trainline booking technology or the BA app.

Now, most travel-industry apps are absolutely great for booking in nanoseconds. And as a result, the customer gets the impression the app is now reliably running the show and is their main point of contact with the transport brand. Expectations of a whizz-bang-customer-delight experience are now (ahem!) on-track to (er) sky-high levels.

Trouble is, the travel and transport industry in general has only got round to addressing the first part of the transaction. You know, the important part, the one where they capture your credit card details like lightning.

Because most transport apps fall apart a few minutes after the booking transaction completes. Most have no facility for problem solving when something goes wrong. They're not connected to the live-action real world, which is full of fog and snow and malfunctioning credit card terminals and cable-theft and cancelled trains. So the minute there's a problem, the oh-so-handy app becomes *part* of the problem – instead of being a switched-on trusty friend, it's looking a bit blank and repeating itself un-cooperatively. Despite all the imagination and energy that's been invested in innovation, the stranded 21st century customer then has to revert to Victorian technology and queue up at a desk to consult old-school uniformed staff.

This is a brilliant example of seeing the situation only from an in-house perspective. The travel companies knew what they wanted – seamless booking to get the money and commitment off the punters, pronto. They then failed to recognise what their app did to their brand from the customer's point of view. Probably because they didn't ask the customer what their expectations were.

Rule 3 is always include the customers in your Discovery: don't take the business's word for it on their needs, views and their aspirations.

4.   What are the competitors up to?

Competitors used to be something to do with Sales and Marketing. Now, they're our problem. Sorry, I mean "opportunity", to use the correct marketing language.

Your transformation needs to take into account everything you know about what competitors are doing in your marketplace. Ideally, it will put you ahead of the pack; but at Very Worstest you need to be keeping pace.

Marketing folk are trained to look into the empty spaces available in the future – spaces this organisation might claim and fill. They don't think about the now, or the soon: they are programmed to look at the five- and ten-year horizon.

To give an example, in mid-2020 most UK holiday travel companies were in a flat spin about the here and now, desperately filling next week's seats and worrying about ever-changing "air corridors" at the height of the global pandemic. But over in China, the 200-year-old Thomas Cook brand had been quietly purchased by a company who were turning the package holiday operating model on its head. This firm was setting up the new Thomas Cook as an online-only brand, with no infrastructure or risky wholly-owned assets. They were capitalising on the brand and simultaneously de-risking their offer – with an almost diametrically opposed set-up to existing travel providers.

That's the kind of research and thinking we need to do as common-sense thought-leaders – and the kind of space we should be playing in.

5. *Setting out your stall*

Discovery should also build your store. As well as its practical function in identifying the problem statement(s), it should also pique the interest of the business and be part of starting the engagement process. By asking people what would make them more effective and efficient, you're asking them to shape this organisation for the future. That conversation may just start the process of bringing them onside with your Programme.

6. *A minimum viable product*

Your aim in the Discovery stage is to conclude by identifying the minimum viable product (MVP).

The MVP should be extremely clear and not a moving feast. Upping – or downing - the requirements mid-way will lead to disaster and failure to deliver what the business needs. Clarity on the MVP will help you avoid the temptations of bells and whistles; or alternatively mission crop. It will help you plot timescale. And it will tell you if you need to start planning to include scary stuff, such as in-yer-face behavioural change. With a clear MVP, you will know the parameters and scope of your project from its very earliest days.

Listen and learn - key skills and activities for Discovery

Discovery is not about having all the answers. It's primarily about unearthing all the problems and understanding where we are starting from. Therefore, the skills' requirements are as follows:

Open your mind

Discovery has to be done with an open mind. No-one should be on the discovery team if they have already agreed the answer to problems that have not yet been identified. Yes, you are working to requirements and objectives, and you may even know what the core technology problem is when you start: but these must be offset against identifying the truth of precisely where we're starting from; and where the organisation wants to get to.

Discovery could well suggest a completely different solution than what you were mulling over at first...

Two ears, one mouth

As my Nan always used to say, there's a reason God gave you two ears but just one mouth. She should probably have mentioned the two eyes as well.

I suspect that like many people, you are neither perfect nor psychic. Therefore, you do not have all the answers and you do not know all the facts. Consequently, the only way you can arrive at answers is to obtain facts and ideas from other people. You need to understand what other people believe and what they know.

As a result, you will need to listen and observe. The methodology for doing this will depend on your Programme but as an example, at the start of one major transformation programme, my team sat down with 45 people to listen to what they knew and thought. We collected together honest and un-interpreted feedback of their views; and then put together a slightly smaller user-panel to develop the thinking further. We asked and listened – and that gave us a method for creating the true problem statement.

That listening built both relationships and our credibility as a solution-provider. It meant that solutions were practical, intuitive, achievable and all that obvious stuff that can get forgotten. And it gave us cues and clues about how to express our sell-in messages to make them meaningful for all our various audiences.

Discovery is definitely a case for silence being golden. In the beginning, you're there to listen, not to tell people your ideas or impress them with your knee-jerk solutionising (because hey, you can always do that later...).

Count things

If you don't know where you were when you started, you won't know how good your transformation has been when you finish. You need to measure where you are at the beginning on critical tasks and parameters – so you can compare and contrast once your business improvements are in place. Open your ITIL Handbook or find yourself a Big Book of Benchmarking for more information.

Watch the wider horizon

Discovery is not just about identifying what works pre-launch. People often forget the "lifetime" aspects – how the solution will age; how the business might change; or what the cost of a licensed solution might be across the lifetime of its usage. There's no point in short-term thinking and here-and-now perspectives that lead you to solutions that work on Day 1 but become unaffordable or unnecessary or unattractive within two years.

Keep the longer and wider horizon in your sights. Be sure to ask questions that elicit where the organisation/sector/discipline is going, to anticipate future needs, opportunities and budgets.

Just ask! Some Discovery tips and techniques

One of the greatest benefits of Discovery is that it tells you which *kind* of transformation you need. Here, I don't mean whether you need a revamp or a reinvention: I am making the point that no two transformations are identical. The *operating principles* are exactly the same – e.g. robust governance, huge and careful attention given to communications, time spent on truly engaging everyone – all that stands the test. But…

….Every single transformation has different points of emphasis. Each has a different context, specific challenges and needs a particular tone of voice. Discovery needs to uncover this – not just identify what kit they use in Finance or whether the CRM system is up to snuff.

Therefore, I've drawn up a basic Discovery Checklist which can be used as a starting point. Of course, you will need to customise it to fit with your parameters, but as a starter-for-ten this should get you thinking about what else you'll need to know:

Questions to ask (of) the C-suite

- **What went wrong last time?** I always start with the negative – it gets so much more honesty at high speed. The question might be tailored around the specifics – such as "What are the key shortcomings of what we have now?" or "Where are your expectations not being met?"

Make it clear you are asking for the warts-and-all bad news – EVEN IF you personally were the author of some of the existing unpopular systems. This is not about you – it's about what's best for the business. And it looks impressive if you the guts to ask **everybody** this, not just the C-Suite.

- **Of the C-suite, what percentage would you say have bought-in to this programme? Where within the C-suite are the lower levels of buy-in?** These questions give you a starting point for your engagement campaign. Obviously, you do not go up to each C-Suite member bold-as-brass and ask "Hey Barry, you bought-into this or what?". Two ears, two eyes, no mouth.

- **Characterise the appetite for risk in a) your CEO and b) the rest of your C-suite.** When you have the answer, you can choose to view it as a constraint; or instead, a primary strand of your communication campaign. You can ask them this or deduce it from their other statements and actions. Asking them would be wiser, as it is puts it on the record.

- **How would you describe your previous change initiatives from the five words and phrases offered below?**

  - ➢ Top down
  - ➢ Refreshing
  - ➢ Collaborative
  - ➢ Chaos
  - ➢ Evolutionary

  Respondents are only allowed to select one word or phrase – and the choice is deliberately not "either/or". This will give you the tone of how they *feel* about previous experiences of change.

- **How did the organisation set the time-frame/deadline for the completion of this change?** Surprisingly arbitrary timelines are often set – so it's best to check early on just how real and reasonable to window is.

- **Is this the only significant change programme we will be running in the assumed time period – or will we have any other major initiatives ongoing?** "Other" includes, for example, mergers/acquisitions or other C-suite led initiatives such as culture change programmes. A complex suite of changes happening simultaneously is not impossible – but meticulous co-ordination of communications will be essential.

Questions to ask (of) the Divisions

- **How would you describe your previous change initiatives from the five words and phrases offered below?**
  - ➤ Top down
  - ➤ Refreshing
  - ➤ Collaborative
  - ➤ Chaos
  - ➤ Evolutionary

- **Is this the only significant change programme we will be running in the assumed time period – or will we have any other initiatives ongoing in this division?** As well as the company-wide initiatives addressed above, it is very common for divisions or sub-groups of people to be running other changes – for example, organisational restructures, plant upgrades or product launches. These will give you information on how much attention this division will give to your Programme; whether there is a potential for conflicting changes; and whether arms will be opened in welcome. Again, this will inform your plans for engaging their involvement.

- **What technology do you have now?** What precisely does it do for you? Where does it fall down? How does it waste time? Where is it? Who uses what? Do you own it or hire it from Microsoft et al? What supplier relationships are in place?

- **What processes do you follow now?** Are these dictated by the technology, or is it the other way round? Which processes are noticeably cumbersome/time-wasting? What characterises process improvements that have worked really well in your Division?

- **How do people in your Division abuse the technology and the processes?** Why do you think they do this?

- **How do your technologies and processes link-up with those used by other Divisions (or Departments)?** Where are the gaps and broken links?

- **Where are the opportunities to be bigger, smarter, faster, more?**

Questions to ask (of) the Users

- **What is inefficient, frustrating, broken?** Why do you say this? Here, you will need to observe, probe and evaluate, as well listen. For example, it could be that frustration comes from an ill-advised process rather than unsuitable technology – or vice versa.

- **How could we help you do a better job?** You can prompt with ideas for time-savers, step-removers or customer-satisfaction-enhancers.

- **Where are the opportunities to be bigger, smarter, faster, more?**

Questions to ask (of) the customers

- **What do our competitors do better than us? Where do we exceed what is on offer from our competitors?** This is a bit risky, because it might raise expectations that you will definitely deliver whatever they mention. Only ask this question if you're intending to knock your competitors' offer into a cocked hat (whatever a cocked hat is). If this feels too out-there, you could always try....

- **In a perfect world, what else could we do to impress you? In the real world, what one thing would you like to see improved?** Again, this line of questioning needs careful management in order to keep expectations realistic – hence the careful wording. You might consider investing in external, professional and neutral facilitators for customer Discovery.

Questions to ask (of) everyone

- **What will success look like?** This is the question to ask of everyone you meet. Obviously, you'll make sure the executive sponsor answers this, but don't forget to ask every manager and end-user you encounter, too. You'll be surprised how much the answers will interlock.

Look 'em right in the eye

One last point on Discovery. Just to be clear, I'm talking about putting in the hard yards here. Yes, you *could* elicit information using internal paper or electronic surveys and suggestion schemes. You'd be able to collect a large number of perspectives. Those who cared could take part and you'd possibly get a broad and in-some-places deep assessment.

But I would much more strongly recommend face to face dialogue. Human conversation is far better at getting first the headlines, and then probing to get to the bottom of problems and suggestions. This will go a long way to building a clearer picture of what your colleagues *need* vs. what they *want*. It helps you see behind the surface requirements to any underlying agendas; and helps you understand how two people can perceive the same situation with diametrically opposed responses. With front-line access and the ability to ask questions, you can sort out the false-positives and the contradictions.

The time and effort will always prove worthwhile. As well as getting to the heart of problems, you will also be building relationships with key stakeholders and starting their engagement with your Programme. They will feel loved and listened-to.

And a bit of good news: you don't have to do it all yourself. Using unstructured questionnaires, intelligent Business Analysts and some Good Old-Fashioned Good Listeners can add speed and capacity to your squadron of information-gatherers.

In Case of Emergency, Break Glass

Protecting the Empire

Discovery only works if people will tell you things. It can be quite common for poorly engaged colleagues to keep all their information close to their vests. These are people who believe they have empires to protect; who do not welcome your "interference"; and who do not want to their way of doing things to change.

This situation requires a Bad Cop, Good Cop pincer movement.

Happily, you get to play Good Cop. You will first need to work harder at engagement. Begin by going back to basics and selling-in the benefits of your programme to this Empress, preferably couched in Empire-preservation concepts that will resonate. Explain how it is in her own best-interests to co-operate with the Discovery exercise.

Simultaneously, tee-up your Sponsor to play Bad Cop. This person will need to have a conversation with the C-Suiter to whom the reluctant person reports. Your Sponsor will need to seek that leader's help to engage our Empress. I suggest your Sponsor provides the other C-Suite member with ideas to describe why it is not risky to co-operate with the process.

The very fact that the senior team has become involved in the conversation is usually enough to change resistant minds. So as Bad Cops go, you're really only asking your sponsor to be Columbo, not Jack Regan.

7. Journey of a thousand miles

Getting started

You have your problem statement and information on your operating context. You now need to plan. Or maybe act.

It can be difficult to know quite what to do first when all eyes are turned on you, waiting for you to show and tell them how you're going to fix it. There's no need for this stage to be as daunting as it sounds. The key to getting started on transformation is to plan AND act – then you please all your audiences. Here's what I'd recommended for the first 90 days:

The ten-step plan

The journey of a thousand miles begins with a single step. That's how you have to look at getting started if you are to avoid paralysis by worrying about everything that needs doing. But what do you do after that first single step? Well: here's that first step and nine further paces...

1. Reality check

You have your Discovery results. You are now in a position for an early-doors Reality Check. Given what you've identified in Discovery, have you *really* got the right brief? It could be that you've been hired to fix something that is **or is not** broken. Get that straight in your head, so that you're 100% crystal, watertight, dead-cert clear on what you stand for, what you've promised and what has to happen at headline level. And at this stage, you will need to start managing expectations about what we are doing/can do/will do, now you know what the reality is.

To get aspirations and expectations in check, you will then need to….

2. Set and communicate a vision and a blueprint

Your vision is a bit like a political manifesto. It tells people what they can expect of your Programme, but by selling the sizzle and not the sausage.

Eh?

Apparently "sell the sizzle and not the sausage" is an old advertising adage, which says that persuasion is achieved by bringing to life the attractiveness of the sausage – it's sizzling tasty appeal – rather than discussing the rather worrying ingredients of a processed meat product.

Using this meat-based model, you will need to persuade people by causing them to imagine a world that includes the benefits of this transformation. That's the equivalent of the tempting sizzle. They will have, for example, more real-time accurate data on which to base their decisions; or one intuitive interface that does everything; or much faster transaction time – bring to life whatever the benefits are. In the vision, they do not need to know precisely how you will achieve these benefits – that would be the what's-in-the-sausage sausage part. Let's not go there.

Alongside the vision, you will need to devise and communicate a plan. For public consumption, the type of plan you need is best described as a "blueprint". It is neither necessary nor advisable to communicate the entire project plan to all colleagues – it just becomes an oh-so-tempting opportunity for debate and revision, which is an excellent substitute for Real Work. Brief people and departments on a need-to-know basis, at the time when they need to hear it.

Your published plan needs only the headlines of what will be happening and when. That's enough rope. What Steve Jobs said about "clean thinking" comes in here (as it does in most areas of transformation):

"Simple can be harder than complex. You have
to work hard to get your thinking clean to make
it simple. But it's worth it in the end because
once you get there, you can move mountains."

With this in mind, a key component of the blueprint is a
statement of the Programme's purpose. Refining that
statement of purpose so that it communicates to all readers in
nanoseconds is worth spending time on. Because if the
purpose of the Programme is clearly understood, it's so much
easier for everyone in the organisation to understand what's
in and what's out – and to more readily adopt the changes
involved.

3. Deliver some early wins
It never hurts to make people feel better, ASAP. So go for
some early wins at this stage. Identify those things that will
need to change, come what may.

Top Tip: a good place to gain these wins in is the leadership
team – what quick fixes can you do for this team to begin
positive engagement with the VIPs? It's essential to show
people that something is happening, even if it's only a tiny-
but-clever little something-ette.

As an example, I was once required to win over a technophobe C-suiter, who had experienced low satisfaction with IT and who had very little time available to engage with me. However, he was *really* interested in real-time knowledge of share prices. It took less than half a day to get him a wall-mounted screen devoted solely to FTSE foibles. The technology chosen was academic and even irrelevant, but the benefit was hugely valuable to him. He was then inside the Programme tent. We now had a positive and buildable relationship.

So where's your opportunity for gaining engagement whilst/by improving the organisation? Fashion insiders say that invisible mikes for Zoom and Teams are trending on the IT catwalk this season...

4.   Hire the first A Team

Then, hire the A-team. That's right: you don't do this all by yourself, because you personally will not know enough about the breadth of subjects you'll need to consider. Instead, you'll be needing a hybrid squadron of true subject matter experts to help deliver the programme. The A Team includes whatever technology honchos are applicable as well as the A Team described in Chapter 10.

5. *Do your due diligence*

You need the A Team in place before you do your due diligence, as they will be able to ask the right questions, pick at the scabs and then tell you how it really is. They'll know their stuff well-enough to spot where you're being flannelled; where the organisation hasn't recognised its weaknesses (or, quite often, its strengths); and where the pressure points of the programme will be. You are going to need boffins who are independent of both key suppliers and the organisation; and can assess everything from technology to marketing practice to law to strategy to leadership culture.

6. *Choose your Target Operating Model*

Decide on what you need. Choose your Target Operating Method and type of supplier(s), if required. Use your A-team to select the perfect TOM from Dick and Harry. Use their excellent noses for bovine effluent to help you pick the right (style of) supplier. Just a thought here; you can only do a good job of this if you've done well on Step 5. But equally, if you have done your due diligence well, decisions come fast and easy...

7. *Request for Information/Request for Proposal*

Only now will you know if you might need to buy something. Therefore, it's time to start the dreaded beauty parade of suppliers. Top tips here include....

a) Try to avoid it, if you possibly can! A beauty parade is extremely time-consuming and not always enlightening. So, contrary to most received wisdom on procurement, I'd say that if you have a dead-cert capable firm, then use them, and don't waste the time of other contestants who you're only planning to disappoint, anyway. You can move straight to negotiation with your preferred supplier.

I would even go so far as to say that you shouldn't worry too much if the supplier isn't provably-perfect, as long as you trust that they have the right level of quality and the willingness to stretch themselves. When there are very high levels of trust in place, it is very likely that a smaller supplier will rise to the occasion and deliver in a scaled-up fashion. The key requirement is that you truly believe in the quality of that supplier.

b) In the absence of a known supplier, take recommendations from people you know, as this will shortcut the exercise enormously. Don't be afraid to ask colleagues for their experiences – including war-stories of where it all went horribly wrong. Other routes to a good quick shortlist include checking out who the competitors use; and of course, firms who have credible evidence of having done this very thing before.

c) Try to keep the investigation – Request for Proposal – down to two candidates. Your aim should be to get depth of information rather than breadth, and really understand what each supplier can and cannot provide. It takes time to do that thoroughly.

d) Don't be afraid to give full information to the supplier-candidates. First, put time into creating a comprehensive brief and then follow up by answering supplementary questions generously. Briefing suppliers well removes misunderstandings – and verbal punch-ups – further down the line. I'm always nonplussed when buyers keep that information secret: this is an exercise in getting the best for your Programme, not an exam for psychics!

e) Live within your means: and buy a good Merc rather than a rusty old Maserati. Clearly identify the budget you can realistically afford from the start. Then, look for suppliers in the top-tier of what you can afford – rather than the bottom tier of what's ritzy but, if we're honest, a bit beyond your wallet. The De Luxe provider will only give you a poor service, because you'll never be their VIP.

   Think creatively and bravely. For example, don't worry about cultural barriers if you can only afford offshore or nearshore. These services will often offer really good quality and value.

8. More quick wins

Now it's time to go for some momentum-gaining quick wins, before anything gets properly underway. So make something that's really rubbish instantly better for the team – as long as it sits within the scope of what you'll be doing overall. Again, it reassures everyone that something is happening, as we're probably getting very near the end of Month 3 by now, and the change-curve grumbling will be thunderous. So buy some printers or some software licenses; or give everyone two screens or a laptop; whatever. The only rule is that it MUST be something that you would be buying, come what may.

9. Hire the second A-team

Now you need to hire/select a second A-team. This is *not* by any means the B-Team – it really is another A-team selected with different criteria! This A-Team-2 will be your bridge-team of experts who will connect, oversee and quality assure what any suppliers will be providing with what the organisation wants and needs. They'll each be very expert, perhaps in software or risk or culture or law, but always in de-flannelling. They may or may not be the same people who did the due diligence – but they'll probably be a larger number of people than A-Team-1. One thing's for certain: they are not YOU. Get them started by unpicking and stress-testing anything the suppliers offer.

10. Take hold of the reins

Finally: you're ready to start. It doesn't matter that you are not the Expert Guru of Everything – your other people are all 10th Dans in their own field and they'll keep you straight. You just have to marshall them; keep a watching brief on how it's all fitting together; and keep your clearly-focused eyes on the prize.

In Case of Emergency, Break Glass

On the Starting Grid

Blockers to getting started come from all angles. Programmes can get stalled by budget wrangles; product launches; business cycles; culture programmes ... it sometimes feels as though every single part of the organisation can give you a great reason not to start.

If you are seeing major obstacles, I'd recommend a three-step approach:

- **Check the position carefully**: it's often the case that some progress can still be made. Don't start anything on a whim, always do a detailed risk analysis first. However, it could be there's an opportunity to work on some preparatory stages.

- **Start somewhere else**: instead of running with your planned sequence, it may be possible to start the Programme in a different place. Again, however much you're chomping at the bitt, check first with the leadership team, via your sponsor, that your Plan B is acceptable.

- **Keep smiling**: because you may just have to grin and bear it. Park your own frustration and get over yourself, however irritating it is not to be allowed to crack on. As steward of the Programme, it is essential that you stay positive about the initiative and the organisation, especially at this tone-setting stage in the proceedings. If your head goes down now, you may never recover credible leadership of the Programme.

8. How not to drive a Sinclair C5

De-risking transformation

You want to deliver the transformation your organisation needs. Of course you do. But no transformation is without enormous risk, as many CIOs (think banking!) know to their cost.

So how do you keep the risk of disaster as low as possible? How do you keep it on track, managing any expectations that have got out of hand? How do you avoid sub-optimal delivery caused by a surfeit of caution? And how do you avoid creating the most embarrassing white elephant in the room?

Great expectations

When *I* was a lad, telephones were indoors and connected to the wall with a bit of string. All telephoning, especially calls indicative of romance, was strictly supervised and frequent reminders were issued about the prohibitive costs involved.

Then the technology changed. By the early/mid-Nineties, phones could be taken anywhere – even into the next room! By the end of the 90s, more than half the population had this facility. By 2005, almost everyone did. Calling was now cheap, even free. Work could now be conducted in almost any space on the planet. Workers could be contacted at almost any time of the day. By the pandemic of 2020, almost all office work could be carried out off-site.

Telephony is perhaps the most obvious way in which the arrival of technology took the lead in changing the way we work. But it's also taught everyone in the Western world about technological advancement. Oh, how we smile about phones the size of house-bricks with pull-up aerials. Or the snap-shut cool-dudery models c2000. Or the revelation that was The Blackberry. But the rapid evolution of the phone has made technology's potential for adaptation or reinvention very visible to the workforce. People now expect - as standard -continuous evolution and transformative capabilities from technology. Not surprising, because as consumers they are offered re-engineered phones, doorbell apps and AI kettles in every ad-break.

The whole population now knows that technology can be made to evolve rapidly. Therefore, we all simply expect that the necessary technology will be waiting in the wings to deliver any workplace specification that we can dream up. Expectations of content and speed are incredibly high.

For the Transformation Lead, this can present a minor migraine. The business will identify a business need within the Programme and then someone is bound to say: "surely there's already an app for that?". There is an expectation that technology moves so rapidly that anything that doesn't already exist can be built smoothly and swiftly.

In this situation, it's the Transformation Lead's job to:

- First and foremost, deliver what the business needs
- Take ownership of that innovation and delivery
- Manage expectations of what can be done; and by when…

… and all that with no loss of credibility.

Therefore, I'm offering the following checklist for de-risking transformation when your business assumes that anything – and everything – is possible within your transformation…:

1) Check that everyone now believes in the vision
Chapter 7 covers putting on your visioning hat and setting a clear direction. While your quick wins are progressing, you have a good opportunity to check that your vision is embedding.

I will always check this informally. Strolling casually round the building and whistling jauntily, I will engage people from all parts of the organisation in conversation about the Programme. I ask them what they expect it will deliver *for them*. Of course, it is especially important that the vision is shared and signed-up-to amongst the top few layers of the leadership of the organisation. That is a dressing room that must not be lost.

If the gist of the answers I get (though not necessarily the vocabulary) encompasses the vision, then I know it has stuck. If their answers are all over the place, we need more work. Because that means they still have their own ambitions and agendas; and we do not yet have a unified understanding and shared expectations.

A note here: embedding the vision when it hasn't taken root is not just your job as Programme Lead. Yes, you are very important in repeating the message. Yes, skilled Communications people will be able to help. But real opinion shift will be most likely to happen if everyone in your team is briefed to communicate what the benefits of the transformation will be, with everyone they meet.

2) *Make sure the customers are still with us*

The customers, or "service users", or whatever you call the people who need the outputs of your organisation, should be the key beneficiaries of your Programme. I've banged on already about the importance of collecting their views and requirements.

But risk creeps in very quickly around the topic of "customers".

The first problems arise if other parts of the organisation become protective about customers: "They're ours" say Sales. "If *you* talk to them, you'll only go and upset them."

Sales are right, of course, to an extent. It is a very dainty path you need to walk to discuss your offer with customers without inviting criticism or raising expectations you cannot fulfil. That's why I would advise using skilled professional intermediaries to have the conversation with representatives of the customer base. But you'll still need to sell that to Sales.

Involve Sales – or any other resistant colleagues – in the discussions about how the customers will be approached and reassure them about how expectations will be managed. Be entirely transparent about what will be discussed and what will happen if customers express negative opinions or frustration. Persuade them of the benefits of being seen to listen to the clients. And always, before you approach any customers, make sure resistant colleagues are on your bus.

Other customer-centred problems can arise when you are using particular delivery methods. Imagine the scene: you consult with the customers; they state their expectations; you assure them that these can be included in your programme. Fireworks, champagne, rejoicing. And then you select a waterfall development mechanism with the supplier sitting way outside the business and producing phased development that takes weeks, or months, or even years. Customer delight = zero.

This isn't necessarily solved by changing your delivery method to suit one stakeholder – yes, agile delivery may produce quicker visible results, and that would be attractive here. However, you nonetheless need to balance your decision with other significant considerations (e.g. budget, culture, capacity) and use the method that's best overall for your stated purpose. So if it's going to be a while, you need to manage customer expectations. Ask your Communications Team to set up a plan *with Sales* on how we keep customers excitedly patient.

3) *Get to the truth behind the statement*

Kids in a sweetshop. To some extent, that's what rapidly evolving technology has made us. We get dazzled by the new and we want it now. Some people want everything that's new, simply because it's, well... new. This can lead to the business attempting to dictate the technology solution to the transformation team.

So the first step is to identify how genuine the need is to the business. Is it a real need, giving us an edge with our customers or in our sector? Or is it just a whim; or perhaps a knee-jerk ticking of the box on technological innovation? Something the initiator wants to flash around in the pub or put on her CV?

Discovery should uncover a goodly portion of this, but always keep checking as we go, to get to the truth behind the statement. Ask open questions of those people who are stating that we have this need. Why do we need it, what will it do for the customers, where will we use it? Check how robust this idea is. If there's lot of on-the-hoof response, don't rush into any action – instead move to quantifying the need/benefit first.

4) *Define what success will look like*

There's nothing riskier for transformation than "blue sky thinking" – both the idiotic phrase and the activity. Specifically, I mean the act of a lot of people imagining completely new things, independently of each other.

There will have been senior-level discussion of what the transformation will do; what it will look like; and what results it will achieve. However, it's likely that each member of the leadership team is using a slightly different paradigm. Therefore, they will all have a slightly different view of the new opportunity and solution. Someone needs to capture these varying visions and expectations.

For the avoidance of doubt, before commissioning any work, I recommend sitting down with each of them individually. Draw up a list of what they each imagine the transformation and technology will add, and how it will have to work for everyone to believe it is worthwhile. When you ask people to demonstrate the tangible outcomes they want, they will often communicate more clearly about their expectations. You will have a more detailed picture of what the transformation needs to deliver.

5) Understand how people will use it

Why has no-one come up with an app for herding cats? People would really use that. Someone could make a lot of money from designing it.

The people who will use our transformed processes and technology are a herd of cats – even in the hyper-obedient corporate world. They will not use these for their true purposes and in the prescribed ways unless it feels right and is easy.

Therefore, the next step is to collect information on how people carry out the affected task(s) now; how they break the rules; what they skip; and how they corrupt processes by what they do. It won't give you a cat-proof blueprint, but it will at least ensure the cats sniff it in the first place. You can then build-in craftier workround-prevention.

6) Don't reinvent the wheel

There's something about those Silicon Valley rockstars that seems to make people want to be first-to-production with a new New Thing. Maybe it's the megabucks; maybe it's the polonecks, but lots of people are a closet Steve Jobs.

For most of us, the truth is that our transformations will not need bleeding-edge technological advancement. Of course, everyone wants to out-run obsolescence but it's essential not to be diverted by hot-off-the-press technologies and solutions. They're sexy, sure – but are they what this business really needs?

I learned early that the newest solution isn't by definition the best. Instead, it's essential to balance the technology specification, design and build against those business benefits we truly need. So if the business needs bells but not whistles, don't be tempted by whistles, just because they're there.

The rule for selecting technology has been: does it benefit the customer? If it doesn't benefit the customer directly, does it help the smooth running of the business (which in turn will benefit the customer in the long run)? This question-sequence is invaluable in helping select a suite of technologies that perfectly fit the Programme's stated needs. And only change business processes where this improves customer service and/or operational efficiency. Common sense.

So don't reinvent the wheel. Instead, look along the shelf of existing products first, and buy, customise or adapt something that already exists. It will save time and cost, both of which gain internal approbation. Wandering round the stage wearing a Madonna-mike is over-rated, anyway.

7)   Get the best out of the people who'll get the best out of the technology

You might not have the in-house skills to develop or customise the technology you need. If that's the case, do not attempt to Blue-Peter-it and run one up in the garage from old washing up liquid bottles and sticky back plastic. It's almost always a false economy. Buy in whatever extra expertise you need.

Consider using near-shore developers to help. I've bought-in some excellent software development from within the EU in recent years. I believe one of the massive advantages of using this type of near-shore development is the opportunity it presents to develop the product using hybrid teams – in-house people working alongside experts from the partner company. Ideas are cross-pollenated; both parties develop their own knowledge, techniques and IP; and the absolutely-right product is developed at an accelerated rate.

8) *Evangelise about agile*

Agile development is well-worth considering to de-risk the programme by engaging the business with the transformation and its solutions.

Agile is sometimes seen as "they've launched it before it was ready". Again, that comes from a Noughties mindset which believes that technology and process change are imposed upon the business by The Faceless Them.

As transformation leaders, we need to educate colleagues that agile development is in fact a collaborative form of developing the right technological solution. It's building the process and the product with the feedback woven into it – and it's NOT imposing "a half-baked solution that IT haven't fully tested".

By gaining colleagues' acceptance of agile development as the best way of quickly incorporating the end-user's ideas, needs and feedback, we can reverse this unhelpful perception and engage users much more closely. And as every transformation lead knows, if you engage their interest before go-live, they are so much more likely to use it effectively post-launch.

9) *Fail fast*

Fail fast – but don't call it that!

Of course, agile development assumes that the product will not be perfect first time and will need adaptation. It will, technically, fail at first. Failure is good – it gives invaluable information on precisely what is not right and needs to be adjusted. Early failure means there's still time to amend and evolve what we're working on.

Failing fast is an excellent step in a rapid development process. It's just that the language is unfortunate – people natural see the word "fail" as negative. So be sure to use the language of "trial" and "prototype" and "model" and "pilot" and "proof of concept" ... Officially, you're not failing fast; you're taking your prototype to V.2.

10) Eyes on the prize

Back to Steve Jobs. And the Zuckerberg guy. These people made a few bob selling their ground-breaking concepts to a global audience. A number of CEOs will have read books about them – or as a minimum, seen the movies. And any CEO worth her salt will always be looking for the best return on her investment.

So the CEO who puts those two ideas together will soon be asking how we monetise our investment. Is there a market for what we're inventing here? Can we potentially sell it to partners, competitors, or people in entirely dissimilar industries?

It's a legitimate question; and very occasionally, there might be more money to be made from the new technology than there is from continuing with our mainstream business. But that will only occur *very* occasionally. So by all means investigate the opportunity; and partner with Marketing to look at the potential, but keep your eyes on the prize.

Persuade the CEO that our own use of the transformational technology will be its proof-of-concept and that perfecting it for our use first is an essential starting point, prior to monetising it. The alternative – very quickly developing a catch-all product that suits other users or industries – is risky. First, any launch would be weakened without a successful proof-of-concept. Second, the hybrid or homogenous version we would create may not be the best fit for our own original purpose.

This is just one example of the distractions that surround transformation and cause mission creep. Good governance and a weather-eye on the minimal viable product will keep you sticking to the knitting.

11) Create appetite

Do you remember, about half a chapter ago, I mentioned involving the users of the technology and processes? That's something that happens very early in the transformation journey. And so by the time of launch, those users may well have let the idea slip their minds.

Therefore, it is always worth de-risking by deliberately creating some increased appetite for the innovation before it goes live. Only people who believe in it will use it.

I recommend creating some communication partnerships – such as Sales/Marketing for communicating with the customers; or the line managers of the people in the organisation who will be using it day-to-day. Understand from these partners what the likely barriers to incorporating this innovation are going to be. Tee-up the partners to start work on energetically communicating what's going to be better. NB. That's "better", not "different".

Make sure everyone in these communication chains understands what the benefits are of the new technology and processes. These people need to be able to answer everyone's favourite question: "What's in it for me?" Because no-one likes change. They say they do, but actually at best it's inconvenient and an effort. At worst it's a scary threat. And there's no natural appetite for being inconvenienced, worn-out, threatened and scared. So you have to make it worth it.

12) Make sure it gets used.

See above for carrots. Now: sticks.

By the time of launch, you will have invested a considerable chunk of time and money into your transformation. Just like, once upon a time, Clive Sinclair did with his Sinclair C5.

Do *you* drive a C5? Thought not. This vehicle represented a revolution in behaviour and technology that we wholeheartedly failed to embrace. Sinclair had used leading edge design and content; he'd partnered well; he'd communicated widely on the benefits of the new machine. But we didn't buy it. Literally.

Any transformation can easily go the same way. Therefore, you may be wise, as a leader of your business, to use a tool that Sinclair did not have available to him: coercion.

Full and proper use of new technology and processes can be very effectively encouraged by making competence one of the objectives/KPIs by which staff performance is measured. Failure to use the technology, or partial/improper use, will reduce an individual's scores-on-the-doors at year end. Or perhaps their non-compliant use will show in their performance statistics – they're just not getting the results the others are achieving. Whichever way you do it, be sure to measure the adoption of the new technology and processes within the employee performance evaluation tool your firm uses.   It sure focuses attention...

In Case of Emergency, Break Glass

Accepting Risk

Of course, it's only common sense to remove the maximum amount of risk from your transformation. However, zero risk is not an option. You can never take away all the possible downsides, however much instinct drives you to want that.

Consequently, it can be the case that you have put a lot of thought and effort into de-risking, but you are still not comfortable. This "*Break Glass*" offers some suggestions for analysing and accepting your position on risk.

- Are you finding research or cross-checking extremely attractive at the moment? If so, this could be a displacement activity, rather than careful risk-minimisation. If you persuade yourself you need more information, you may be giving yourself a "good reason" for not taking the decision to begin. Fear is your "real reason". Ring a bell?

- Or have you suddenly become very keen on engagement activities? Again, you may not be de-risking but procrastinating. Further engagement will come by delivering the programme, not by talking about delivery.

117

- What's your instinctive decision-making approach? Those people who use "take a decision; if it's wrong I can simply take another one" are not even reading this section. Think about your historic patterns of decision making and decide whether these are useful.

- Don't know where to start? Just pick a small task from the list and do it. That'll warm you up for the bigger tasks. Don't attempt to start with the cliff-face actions such as strategy development – they're too daunting. Limber up first.

- Set a phoney deadline. Promise someone something from the Programme for next Monday. Obligation is an excellent driver.

9. Ground control and Major Tim

The importance of governance

On any Digital Transformation Programme, good governance is imperative. You need it for a multitude of reasons – from reassuring the project sponsor to keeping your own team on track. It imposes discipline which will support your own self-discipline; and indeed it keeps you safe when something goes wrong, which - believe me - it will. At first, it may feel uncomfortable to put yourself into a weekly spotlight-in-your-face interrogation, but that will prove worth it for the quality of ownership and communication it gives to the Programme.

Keep it light or go in heavy?

There are two schools of thought surrounding governance. One champions light-touch governance, that doesn't stand in the way of progress and creativity. That appeals to me hugely, but I think it belongs in a space that I don't usually inhabit. Light touch governance keeps the juices flowing in smaller organisations, such as start-ups, where there is widespread equality and implicit trust. It works well for self-confident practitioners in organisations that have self-governance and mutual reliance wired into their DNA.

I tend not to work in those environments. I'm far more used to large-scale corporate organisations, often global and dispersed. I'm used to people marking my work who don't really know me. I typically have to put forward work done by my team to people who don't really know them. These types of environment, on balance, seem to benefit more from very rigorous governance, that assures transparency and leaves the leaders of the organisation feeling in control.

By definition, most digital transformations are in established organisations, which in all probability have become larger or more dispersed since their inception. So as a rule of thumb, I'd recommend using conspicuously rigorous governance for these situations. Why?

Why it's worth it: with your sponsors

Programme Sponsors constantly seek reassurance. That's not always just the obvious reassurance that you'll be in budget and on time. They also want to be able to confidently assert that everything is OK when they're challenged – by the Board, or the shareholders, or the staff. Yes, they want to have confidence that it will all happen as planned and on time; but they want to be assured that you've selected the right solutions and taken the right decisions. And the sponsor will not always have the right knowledge to judge your judgements.

They need to believe in you because they'll be the people getting the kicking later if you get it wrong.

Good governance gives them the necessary assurance. It also serves to build a positive relationship between your team and its Executive Sponsor. When it works well, they believe you are being transparent; there is someone else checking your maths; and they believe that any predictions you make will come true.

Ground control and Major Tim

Do you remember that British astronaut bloke? You probably do, but you can't remember his name, though. You might remember that he was a bit ... sensible. He was Major Tim Peake.

Transformation Programmes are like British astronauts – they're not all rock 'n' roll; they're not Buzz Aldrin or Buzz Lightyear. Instead, they're all about the safe, sensible and boring elements that actually create the achievement. Just like in the real-world, astronauts are a lot more Major Tim than Major Tom...

Once, as a significant Programme came close to go-live, I ran a learning exercise with the team to reflect on how we had come to be in the good position we were in. We'd had a lot of fiery hoops to get through and at a rapid pace. We'd had radical ideas; we'd moved the programme to an agile mode from waterfall; we'd appointed new suppliers; we'd developed and tested and refined; but we were ready for lift-off right on time. All good.

However, the team were all agreed that the biggest achievement was the fact that our programme sponsors had been happy to come along on this rocket-fuelled ride. How did that happen? Not because they wanted to have a cutting-edge true digital transformation on their CVs. Not because they fully understood all the finer twiddly-bits of what had been done. Not even because they needed a new system and they wanted it soon. In fact, we identified, they came along with us because they trusted that what we were doing was the right thing. They'd continued to buy-in to this programme.

So why had they continued to strap themselves in and let us fly the rocket? Was it our good relationships? Or perhaps the glamour and sizzle of white-hot IT transformation that had them all fired up? Or our scintillating charm, persuasiveness and charisma?

No. It was something very dull and basic and not rocket science. Robust governance. It was all down to boring old trust, reassurance and security. We would have made no progress *with* good relationships but *without* good governance. We'd put solid ground rules in place: about e.g. decision-making processes; programme content; communication plans; budgets and timing. The framework allowed for changes and setbacks and variable levels of speed of implementation. It had sub-governance structures for each agile work-strand. The progress of the entire programme was independently audited monthly. We talked to the sponsors all the time, making sure we were entirely transparent and honest about where we were against the plans. Dull, dull, dull. Nothing *like* rocket science.

But it had worked. Governance had kept the programme safe and steady.

Why it's worth it: for you and your team

As the lead on any transformation, you need to set your own rules. Any Programme Lead worth their salt will want to be involved in setting the governance criteria and content, ensuring they've brought reason and rigour to the expectations placed on the Programme. But I believe it goes beyond that obvious and logical I-don't-break-the-rules-I-make transaction: it has much deeper psychological and emotional components. For me, these are:

1. **These are not just your rules**. In agreeing the governance criteria with the business, you've psychologically bought-into the business's aims. That often includes committing to massive challenges, like tight deadlines and ambitious multi-project working. You haven't just said you'll do it; you've *promised yourself* you'll do it.

2. **You've agreed the rules on behalf of others**. When you suggested or agreed to certain criteria, you committed on behalf of your team: because you believed this team had the potential to deliver against these demands. You are now obliged to support them to achieve the standards set. You're the cheerleader on their (winning) side.

3. **You need to know you're winning**. Without the rigour of good governance, you can't know if you're ahead of the curve, running to catch up or already standing on the podium. At the end, you can't know if you've done a good job, learned any useful lessons, or have been valued by the people around you. So without rigorous governance, there's no job satisfaction.

I believe that governance setting should be viewed as a leadership exercise in its fullest sense. Yes, you'll be promising the business some tangible delivery and practical outcomes. But that's not the end of it. You'll also need to think more broadly about how you'll be contributing to: improved inter-team performance; the personal performance of yourself and your team members; and the overall quality of the organisation.

Zen and the art of Programme maintenance

So what are these magic rules, then? How do you create a governance structure that reassures the sponsors and keeps you and your team on track? My recommendations are:

You're putting governance in place so that you have an early warning system for something going wrong. If you see the wobble coming, you can fix it before the wheel comes off. In some organisations, governance and governance meetings are a dreaded chore – seen as The Weekly Carpeting (although not always using that last word). Beating up people who have made a mistake in a public place is absolutely NOT what governance is for.

Governance meetings are there to evaluate progress and check we are still on track. They are designed for early problem spotting, leading to early problem solving, which will save the Programme time, money and effort. Full stop.

As any management textbook worth £8.99 will tell you, the best decisions are made by inclusive teams. Where a variety of viewpoints are represented and heard, a decision is more likely to be successful.

Therefore, I'd recommend setting up a governance team representing all parts of the Programme – from all corners of the delivery team, to the suppliers, sponsors and BAU.

Having the programme's executive sponsor on the team is imperative. This person is not a deliverer (except of top-level communication and persuasion) and he/she needs to be there as both the internal customer and intelligent outsider. That makes this person something of a sounding-board/referee. Of course, this is likely to be an extremely busy senior person, so you are going to need all your new-found persuasiveness skills to get him/her there every week.

Make the meeting frequent and regular – every Friday morning is corny but useful. I'd recommend weekly meetings usually. Indeed, weekly is not-negotiable at the start of the Programme when it's exploding in all directions.

Don't be tempted to decrease the frequency of meetings if it's going well – remember this is your early warning system, and the longer the gap between meetings, the less-early and therefore less-useful it becomes.

You'll need to agree some yardsticks and barometers by which you'll measure your progress. There are plenty of obvious ones ("are we still on schedule/in budget?"). The specifics of measures will be unique to your Programme but bear in mind that they are there to help you spot problems arising early doors, so you can give some attention to fixing them.

Think very carefully about what is critical to keep your Programme successful and on the straight and narrow. Collective decision-making by the governance team will be essential here. People buy into the rules they themselves have created.

One reason people groan about governance is that they've been to too many bad governance meetings. Bad governance dwells on detail and poor performance. We've ruled out public stonings already, but what should you do about all that droning on about detail?

First, ban JIRA and spreadsheets. Replace them with a limited system of dashboards that force their owners to summarise the situation before they get into the meeting. Dashboards and simple traffic light systems will give you early visibility of problems. I tend to think of it as a tapestry, little dots of colour making up a whole picture of the progress we're making. As the Lead, you should be only interested in the overview and spotting any impacts coming around the bend.

In the meeting, pay no attention whatsoever to things that are going well. Your team needs to be zen – they won't get a rollicking in this meeting, but equally, neither will they get a paeon of praise. It's not about value judgements, it's about keeping us on track.

The tone is neutral throughout, even though we are now only addressing current snags and looming concerns. This lack of positive or negative emotion reduces the opportunity for stuck parts of the Programme to become political. So don't make it personal; and don't make it critical. The questioning is always based on what precisely the red-light projects need to get them back on track.

You will need to create a safe atmosphere for this meeting. Attendees need to feel they can trust they are in a safe environment, so that they can speak up about their project problems without fear of reprisal or loss of reputation. They have to believe the rest of team is there to, and wants to, help them.

In Case of Emergency, Break Glass

Be consistent: twice

Governance always features a paradox. You need to be consistent: but you also need to amend governance models if they aren't working. To address this, I'd recommend being consistent, but twice. To do this:

1) Begin the Programme by applying whatever governance method has worked for you before on a similarly-shaped Programme. If you're new to transformation, devise a theoretical plan of what *should* work. Choose any permutation (of stand-ups, weekly meetings, written reports, whatever) that seems to fit.

2) Apply the chosen method consistently and see if it's working. Don't change the method time and again or add to the governance burden just so that everything is covered from every angle. And "working" is defined as: "giving you timely insight into problems coming around the bend, so you can fix them".

3) If it isn't working, stop what you're doing and have the confidence to change it.

4) Ask the team what they think *will* work (i.e. give better insight into upcoming issues). Agree with them which meetings/reports/check-ins/scrutiny/dashboards/calendars will give better results.

Work hard to keep the governance process credible. It's not an exercise in blame-dispersal; collective guilt; or death by PowerPoint. So be sure all reports are useful; all attendees need to be there (for the whole meeting); and the topic discussed is always 100% relevant to those present.

10.Star Techs: the next generation of skills

Hiring the right people

People think digital transformation is all about technology. In fact, success comes in some part from selecting the right technology, all of which works when it leaves the factory and is simply a matter of specc-ing and applying it correctly. The greater part of success – and the bigger risk of failure – lies instead with people and their behaviour.

It won't matter how good your strategy and governance and technology are if your team is ropey. Obviously, the team must have the necessary knowledge and experience – and just the overall calibre – to deliver. But I believe it also has to have a certain disposition, too.

I'll talk later about setting the right culture – but I believe you can create most of the right culture by hiring it in, in the first place. I have a few qualities I will always seek when hiring, in addition to relevant technical skills: the team always needs skills for collaboration; communication; motivation; and imagination.

It's also worth taking time to carefully select people for a number of pivotal roles on the programme. Programme leaders get hung up on the key technical positions such as architecture, programme design or security. Of course they're important, but the success of the programme will very often be more the result of really talented people in the boiler room.

Collaborative environments attract the best people

I will always aim to create a collaborative environment on any programme – because collaborative working environments and open co-operation invariably attract the very best people. Here are five reasons why:

Good ideas become great ideas. Collaborative people take an idea, without any envy of the originator and add a bit more to make it a great idea. Collaborative idea-generators are never miffed if people add or tweak their idea - for them, the contribution is perceived as success, support and enhancement, not criticism or repair.

Great ideas become reality. Co-operators are not precious or territorial. If the idea needs to be passed on to someone else for development or realisation, they hand their baby over merrily at the nursery door. Truly excellent people recognise that they personally may not have the skills to actualise the idea and they'd much prefer for it to be as good as it can be.

People share; no-one steals. In the right environment, everyone's contribution is acknowledged honestly. No-one would ever pass-off someone else's idea as their own. So everyone deserving of credit, gets it. And everyone gets back as many good ideas as they put in - as my Nan used to say, fair exchange is no robbery.

There is no Coroner's Court. Similarly, in a positive working environment, there's responsibility but no blame. Co-operative teams that come up against a problem work together to crack on and fix it. They do not spend hours or months attending the Inquest, forensically identifying who caused the problem. Sure, they investigate what went wrong and how to avoid that happening again, but they can't be bothered with finger-pointing and tutting.

Collaborators are communicators. By definition, people who work collaboratively have to be able to clearly express their ideas and intentions. So good communicators are working with other good communicators - and therefore less goes wrong, less gets missed, and things move quickly.

The very best people can get work anywhere... So it's pretty unlikely that they'll ever choose an atmosphere of suspicion, blame, secrets, territorialism or mistrust. Therefore, for me the only choice is to create an open and collaborative culture if you want to attract the best team.

To ensure you hire un-territorial people, make sure there are early-stage interview questions that elicit information on how candidates approach collaborative working. Check with your recruiters what they are planning to ask to identify a co-operative mindset. And don't let them confuse a preference for "working quietly" with an uncollaborative nature. Plenty of people like to work in quiet privacy, but it doesn't mean they're not team players.

Your recruiters are looking for people who are open minded to new ideas; who listen to feedback; and who enjoy building something with other talented people.

More follows on creating collaborative working in Chapter 14, *Running the Team.*

The holy trinity: communication, motivation and innovation

A disposition towards collaboration is an essential for me. But I also look for three further mindsets. I've noticed that if most (I've never achieved *all*) team members are also inclined to communicate, innovate and drive their own bus, we succeed with the least effort.

I'd recommend the following mindsets are what you should be looking for as Programme Lead when you're recruiting. I'd expect your recruitment team to furnish you with candidates who have all the required technical competencies, before you then get involved in the final stage interviews. You'll be interviewing to observe speaking and listening skills; self-reliance and a love of progress.

Specifically:

1. *Communicators (who listen)*

Once consigned to a back-room function that no-one remembered unless there was a crisis, IT is changing. It's now coming down from its windowless tower and mixing-it with the rest of the business. Therefore, we need even more people who can communicate to a genuinely excellent standard. These people need to be able to talk about IT in a way that accommodates the perspective and knowledge of their listeners. That includes knowing what to ask; what to mention; knowing what there's *no need* to mention; and knowing how to explain to a level of depth that is intelligent and meaningful, without the listener taking furtive glances towards the door.

More importantly, they'll need to be listeners first and foremost. You need people who don't even get into any sort of explanation until they've completely exhausted Chapter 1 of the Dark Art of Communication – which is getting people to talk honestly and then really listening to what's being said.

Then they need to be persuaders, evangelists and ambassadors. Because as well as doing their own thing (developing, say, or testing, or budget-keeping, or process re-engineering), everyone on the team should be tasked with communicating about the Programme in a way which creates appetite for it across the organisation. Change management and communication are not the responsibility solely of team members who have those words in their job titles – *everyone* is expected to win hearts and minds.

2. Self-starters

You will always need people who can think for themselves. These are people who have ideas for solutions and innovations: and then follow-up on and come forward with these ideas. And people who can work out what they need to know more about before taking a decision: and then go and find that information. People who are sparked to learn more, just because they're curious. And people who just simply crack-on and get the work out of the door.

That's not saying you want a lot of mavericks. The team members will all need to be born communicators and collaborators (see previous paragraph) so they'll happily keep us all involved with on what they're doing. So I guess I'm saying you want a *team* of mavericks!

The generation that is currently qualifying into IT is one of the least-populous for several decades. So we'll have fewer people to do the doing. That means the people to hire will be the ones who work smarter, get the most done, using the everyday magic of clever-thinking.

3. Imaginative people

Finally you're going to need imaginative people. Not necessarily the IT-obvious-creatives who'd rather be designing games, but simply people who don't assume we have to do stuff the way it's always been done. We know we are in a period of rapid – and possibly currently-unimaginable – change. We're going to need people who can both roll with it **and** see the opportunities it offers.

Then there's empathetic imagination. I also believe we need people who have the imagination - and take the time and make the effort - to understand what it's like to be someone in the business who lives outside the arcane rituals of the IT team. We need people who can create solutions that have at their heart the users' needs, challenges and standpoint.

And they have to be people who see a solution analogously – applying an existing model from another walk of life onto the world they live in. Yes, alright: imaginatively nicking other people's ideas.

You'll notice the list above does not include "people who know about technology". It's not that you're *not* going to need those folks; it's just that this skillset goes without saying. It's the baseline to the other qualities.

The A Team

So who are your key team players? Well, quite obviously, "people who know about technology". Of course, your key personnel will depend on the nature of your programme – but you don't need me to explain that you'll need an A1 AI guru if that's your big opportunity; or a cunning security expert; or sparky developers. The technical roles are usually the easiest to identify, and of course the success of the project is heavily dependent on their skills.

However, I'd argue that there are three more cornerstones to success. I believe a trio of role-groups are critical within the programme, and recruiting for these is often delayed, or hurried, or overlooked, as they are not – at first glance – the stars of the show. But in these three sets, the quality of the individual is pivotal to programme success. So my recommendations for careful recruitment in the three groups are:

Group 1: The trio of Commercial, PMO and Finance

Three very big roles, here. I'm making a point by lumping these three together.

Historically in IT, these roles were traditionally seen as absolutely separate from each other. Indeed, I've experienced projects where there has been downright territorialism and Byzantine empire building, with each lead washing his/her hands of any connected responsibilities that can be passed onto the other folks. That type of approach is hopelessly old-fashioned and culturally chocolate-fireguard-ish. This trio need to work in harness.

I will always hire collaboratively-minded people for these three roles – people who will work together to ensure everything is the team's collective responsibility. This avoids mistakes as tasks fall between two bailiwicks: and even better, it avoids all those hours wasted on forensically identifying whose mistakes the mistakes were….

So what are the other skills and qualities you're looking for here?

Commercial (aka Procurement)
The right relationship with suppliers – "partners" – is critical to the success of the programme. It therefore follows that the right person managing the supplier relationship is also pivotal. Common sense.

My first point on the Commercial role is that this person needs to be hired early-doors. There is no sense in hiring Commercial to pick-over the Swiss cheesy contracts with suppliers that you put in place before the professional arrived on the scene. Hire Commercial before contracting with any supplier.

Next, make sure that the Commercial Manager truly understands partnership working. You need Commercial people to be those who understand that outcomes are agreed with suppliers – and never assumed. My rule of thumb with the client-vendor relationship is that you never have to take the contract out of the drawer. Nothing should arise which makes it necessary to even check The Rules of What We Should Be Getting. We're seeking to create a situation where suppliers – shock! – are allowed to make a reasonable profit from the job and in exchange will always go the extra five miles. So you need a Commercial Manager who has written that into the deal and then – belt and braces – engendered the necessary supplier pride and loyalty to ensure it occurs.

Programme Leads might be tempted to perform this function themselves. If you have the right experience and commercial acumen, you'd probably be suited to it. However, it's important not to underestimate the amount of work it takes to effectively manage supplier relationships – including the dainty detail of contracts, timing plans and SLAs. As Programme Lead, you will have many, many more demands on your time – so as a minimum, get someone in who's good with the teensy-tiny detail and will own the supplier relationship day-to-day.

If I've made you doubt you have capacity/time available, you may prefer to bring in some support to get the very best from the supplier relationships. I'd recommend you look for an experienced Commercial Manager who:

- Works collaboratively with all parties

- In particular, works hand in glove with Finance and PMO, without silos

- Is happy to get close to the detail, day-to-day

- Understands what questions to ask during due diligence, to see through any flannel from prospective suppliers

- Understands contracting and negotiation, *as well as* positive supplier liaison

- Thinks ahead, to ensure the contract is as all-inclusive as possible, to avoid a big bill from later date add-ons and unforeseen premium services

- Takes the long view, looking at the lifetime cost of the Programme so that it continues to be affordable to the business in five years' time. Licenses keep on costing money, people!

- Has a good sense of the commercial landscape, knowing what's for sale and what it's worth...

- ...but nonetheless has empathy for the supplier's position and their need to come away from the experience feeling positive about your organisation

And yes, you're right. I am indeed saying that the days of Procurement being The Office Rottweiler are over. The type of negotiator who insists on nailing the vendor to the table and then laughing in his face is consigned to Gene Hunt World, where they belong.

This is because a contract works best when all parties are happy with it. If either supplier or client feels they are being ripped off, defensiveness creeps in, and then ultimately conflict and frustration. All that takes time away from Getting The Job Done and Doing A Good Job. It's wasted energy.

So you're looking for an intelligent and knowledgeable expert, who sets the tone of the client-supplier relationship right from the stage of drafting the contract. He/she will then Chair "service review" meetings that help guide how the contract comes to life – which is quite an art. Some organisations will run supplier meetings monthly, but I prefer weekly, especially at the start, before there's a chance for things to go adrift.

And there's your first clue about this triumvirate. Quite obviously, those meetings will bring to light financial and project management issues. But these are not to be handed-down from on high to the other teams – they are to be solved by working across. We're all on the same side. Even the suppliers….

PMO

You're also going to need a PMO Lead who can keep both the organisation and the suppliers on-side. PMO is there to work alongside Commercial and keep the output going. In addition, PMO will maintain the quality of what's being delivered. It's quite obvious they can't do this without continuous reference to Commercial.

A good PMO lead recognises that the effectiveness of suppliers is client-dependent. If those of us inside the client organisation don't keep our promises and meet our deadlines, we cannot then expect the suppliers to pick up the slack. So the talented PMO will also persuasively manage in-house expectations and adherence to our obligations as the client.

In addition, PMO has to sidle over to the finance side of the pitch every now and again. It is extremely easy for the business, the Programme sponsors and, on occasion, even the transformation leads and Commercial to get a bit kids-in-a-sweetshop. The vendors come along flashing all the shiny new toys … and mission creep waits just around the corner… PMO needs to be the grown up and pull on the reins. Persuasive diplomacy is an excellent attribute to hire in the PMO.

Finance

Finance completes the jigsaw. In under-developed leadership teams, there is a tendency for PMO and Procurement to dump evaluation-before-payment with Finance. But it's not appropriate for Finance to take time on evaluating output against contract, in a vacuum. It takes close collaboration with the other two to decide when enough value has been achieved for payment to be made. You need a Finance Manager who keeps the dialogue open.

Group 2: Communications and training

The first rule of communications is... you DO talk about communications. Early doors. Communications and training are not something to bolt-on halfway through or towards the launch – you need the messaging managed from the very start.

There's an old-fashioned school of thought that believes talking about the Programme before it's visible and tangible brings it into disrepute; they argue this is promising without delivering. In fact, that's an assumption based on poor communication strategies. In reality, you need to talk about the programme all along – but say different things at the different stages. Therefore, you need Comms on the team – if only with a limited capacity – from the very beginning.

It can be very helpful to involve the Comms team in the Discovery phase. Two reasons:

a) it will help shape the message and manage the (timeline of) expectations
b) they will listen to how the business sees the problem and the Programme. They need that background information to communicate well.

So what are you looking for when hiring for these roles?

You need Communications people who are able to adapt to the reality of the situation. Of course, they need to be persuasive and technically skilled, but they need a very twitchy ear to pick up on the required tone. Therefore, you're looking for:

- People who listen before they speak. The best Comms people sit quietly for a long time, drinking it all in, so that when they respond they pitch-perfectly hit top notes.

- People who can adapt the communication so that it rings-true with each audience. You need people who understand the same message needs to be spun a dozen ways to suit a dozen audiences. Lazy one-size-fits-all communicators need not apply.

- People who explain persuasively but honestly, rather than people who sell. Polishing up the situation to make it more attractive will always be found out. Skilled communicators are those who can make the harsh reality acceptable. Or at least, tolerable and credibly fixable.

And what about the training teams?

For many years, IT thought the best bet for training was to send in the Local IT Expert – the person who knew the most about the relevant piece of software or hardware. That way, any questions that arose could be answered. Stands to reason.

Meanwhile, back in real life, trainees don't actually ask difficult questions about the far end of a farthing functionality of the kit. They don't want an expert: they want a mentor. They want someone to teach and support them as they go through the difficult task of re-learning everything they know about doing their job. Trainees are often in a place where they see the new solution as "slower" and "more work" than their familiar processes and tools. They'll feel frustrated, exasperated and even threatened. Time to be kind.

Consequently, you're looking for trainers with empathy, a supportive attitude and saintly patience. Charm doesn't go amiss, either. And again, it's worth hiring a small training capability early, as prototypes and demos shared with focus groups and UAT volunteers can all be used as part of the engagement campaign.

Which brings me to the final point on this group. As with Commercial, PMO and Finance, try to view Training and Communications as a single entity. Communicators help educate the business; and trainers help the business understand the changes that are happening. The roles overlap and interlock. This team's members may originate from PR and HR – but they need to work on the Programme as a joint enterprise.

Group 3: the Analysts

The analysts are last, but not least. Indeed, the analysts are arguably first, in that – can you believe this? – you need to do (most of) your discovery *before* you commit to buying anything. You need the analysts to gain insight into the business, its needs and its current position before you can start committing to suppliers. Time and again I see digital transformation programmes commit to suppliers, services or products *before* knowing what it is that's really needed. Analyse first!

In this final cluster, I'm including all the people who work with detail, data and information, from the Business Analysts who look at discovery; to the Testing Teams who check that it's working. Traditionally and unkindly viewed as the Data Nerds, the analysts are coming out of the library in modern change programmes. We need them interacting with the business.

Discoverers are here to build the blueprint of facts before we begin. That might be on people or processes, or what shape your data is in. Sometimes, frankly, they even need to go off and discover *where* your data is!

Roles like this have an enormous impact on the success of the Programme – because it's only ever as good as the investigation and checks that it's based on. Therefore, this time you're looking for people who:

- Can identify and interrogate detail. They need to be thorough in doing this...

- ... but still able to deliver analysis in a timely manner. You cannot take any decisions until they've done their work, so skills for balancing content and pace are essential

- Discoverers need to be open-minded, to watch and listen without bringing pre-conceived ideas and solutions to a project. You need people who can interview and facilitate, without bias.

- They need imagination to view the situation from a number of standpoints and lenses, weigh the importance of each perspective and thereby create realistic options for consideration by decision-makers.

- All the analysts also need to be able to build relationships with the business. They are an integral part of the engagement process – from the BAs asking the process owners what functionality they need, to the UAT testers giving it a run out with prospective users. They need to be persuasively on-message and able to build good relationships, part of the team warming-up those people who believe All Change Is A Bad Thing.

No apologies for writing a long chapter on the people doing the job. There is no chance of success without the right people on board. Give your very best attention to recruiting the best team you can find – it will pay you back.

And if you're not able to recruit, but are working with your existing team, more advice in Chapter 14, on running the team.

In Case of Emergency, Break Glass

HR is your friend

There is the potential for Transformation Leads to run into conflict with HR if this relationship is not handled positively. We want to hire quickly, recruiting people with niche skills and often on peculiarly-framed T&Cs. HR want the business to stick to clear recruitment policies and are responsible for maintaining the integrity of the organisation's culture. These two camps could easily come to blows – when in fact it is crucial that we have an excellent relationship with HR.

To avoid any problems, I recommend striking up a positive relationship with the Head of HR very early in your Programme. Explain what you are seeking to achieve with your Programme and its recruitment. Ensure this person is convinced that digital transformation requires an unusual mix of skills, often in atypical temporary arrangements.

Then, support HR as fully as possible in the recruitment process. They are not – and do not claim to be – subject matter experts: but you are. So take the time and make the effort to create a fully detailed recruitment brief.   It's the least you can do for your mates….

11.Howdy Pardner!

A positive relationship with suppliers

IT needs to step away from the old paradigm of beating and bullying suppliers. Because what we all know about bullying is that it's not big and it's not clever. All too often I see people treating suppliers in a negative or hostile way, seeing them as enemies who are out to get us, under-deliver or rip us off. This is just not true of most suppliers. Most are absolutely delighted to work in symbiotic partnership and can be trusted to deliver everything we need – and often far, far more – in order to be allowed to develop a long-term supplier-client relationship. Ask yourself: why *wouldn't* they want that?

Here's my take on how to get the best from a partnership with suppliers – and just a few points that ask any old-school suppliers to have a word with themselves!

Partnership working: first principles for the 2020s

I cut my IT-teeth on dealing with suppliers in the Nasty 90s' world of screw-em-down-then-kick-em-out contracts, but that won't work for me these days. First, most programmes don't need that any more; and second, the big wide world has moved on. Three key principles I work to now are:

1. **Understand that the spec isn't the spec any more.** Many contemporary transformation programmes use fully agile or agile-with-an-end-date development. In these cases, you know where you need to get to. But what you're buying from the developer company is their expertise in *how to get there*.

   Therefore, unlike the olden days, you can't fully spec it. You just have to state the goal. And yes, that means you have to let go of control and trust the supplier to be honest, clever and competent. And that's not just true for development – in this world of fast-evolving technology, the same applies to buying easily-upgraded comms kit for Facilities or helping Marketing teams get the best app solution. So how do we trade like this that without getting stung?

2. **Use Success Contracts.** You always need the right contract for the job. Sometimes that's a humdinger of a Master Service Agreement with 400 pages covering every possibility including what to do in the event of a plague of locusts. But the contract can be equally suitable at a handful of pages. All contracts just need to be clear on two things: a) the required outcome; and b) the option and arrangements for either party to exit the contract if they are not experiencing the required outcome.

With Success Contracts, you get into exactly the same territory as the Pre-Nup. People don't like talking about the escape-hatch-clause when they've just met and it's all very hearts-and-flowers. But dispassionately agreeing a contract that you can terminate if you're not getting what you want is essential. It is both good governance and it assures a good quality of service (oh, and it guarantees well-behaved buyers).

And it means you can relax … and trust them:

3. **Develop trust and transparency.** With a success contract, it's in the supplier's best interests to do a fabulous job. But of course, no contract will really work if there's an imbalance – one side feeling they're not getting a good deal. So there also has to be an utterly transparent relationship. Both parties have to trust each other to deliver. Everyone needs to be clear about how we are sharing responsibility. And there needs to be a fair level of reward. That's not just the old model of "cash for them", but a fair sharing of ideas, innovation and IP. It's a more complex relationship to develop than the old master-slave relationship of buyer-vendor; but it is more productive, more enjoyable, more stable and will last much, much longer….

When I proudly mentioned these rather nifty bleeding-edge ideas to a colleague from Marketing, she started to shuffle away, smiling nervously. When I pursued this, she cringingly explained she'd done all of these things with Coca Cola: but in 1992…. I was reminded that IT is coming late to a lot of practices our colleagues have been using for years. That means we're behind the curve and it's time to catch up.

How partnership working works

Imagine you've bought an Ikea chest of drawers. You've wrestled the flatpack into the car, out of the car and up the stairs. You've now got it in the right room and you can start to assemble it. Your esteemed life partner rocks up. But instead of rolling up sleeves and mucking in, that person simply leans against the doorframe, musing about whether you should have bought one quite that big, giving you ill-informed instructions and criticising how you're doing with the Allen key.

That is precisely the relationship between many IT clients and their suppliers. The heavy lifting and mistake-making is done by the supplier, with the client looking on critically. Neither party enjoys it. The result is rarely quite what either side was looking for. There's no joint enterprise, just a master-slave contract.

In the last few years, I've found that a programme goes so much further so much faster if the whole team genuinely embraces partnership working. That means pooling ideas, knowledge and IP. This can be a little awkward at first if you're coming from the master-slave model. Clients worry about all kinds of things, from where accountability lies; to loss of their IP to competitors; to loss of staff to their suppliers. But I strongly believe that any programme will blossom if everyone signs-up to a few simple rules for partnership working:

1. Be clear about the client

The first step is for all parties to ditch the concept that the purchasing CIO/CTO is the client. I'm not talking about project oversight or accountability (I'm coming on to that), but about the role within the psychological relationship between vendor and buyer.

Everyone involved needs to ask: "who's really the customer?" With new IT, that question can be quite complicated to answer. It might be the end-users within the buyer-organisation. It might even/also be the client's clients. Or both.

What it isn't, in almost all cases, is the Programme Lead/CIO/CTO or the buyer-organisation's IT team. Buyers and vendors who focus on the benefits of their product for the IT people, without regard for down-the-line users, are woefully missing the point.

Vendors obviously recognise the merits of chumming up with the Client IT team. And of course it's beneficial to develop relationships that mean you can all work together smoothly. But suppliers can sometimes get too focused on being the IT Team's mate in order to secure a second sale, even occasionally ganging together against the rest of the client organisation. In fact, the only way they should get a second sale down the line is if their solution is focused primarily on the real client, the end-user. Focusing on the configuration that makes the product easiest for the IT team may not be in the best interests of the organisation as a whole.

So.....

2. Let the business meet the vendors
Vendors are at their most valuable as part of the transformation team when they interface with the wider business directly. Suppliers should be encouraged listen to user feedback, preferably face-to-face, without a lost-in-translation interpreter. They should take time to get an insight into the widest aims of the project. They need to understand what type of business improvement the client is striving for; and what the goals of the full transformation team are. And they should listen: without selling.

IT/Programme Leads can be very nervous about letting this happen. They've often had bad experiences of this in the past.

For example, some suppliers have believed that pantomime demonstrations of competence impress or reassure the business. I once saw a developer showcase his coding skills in front of the end-user's very eyes: "Wow, people! Just *look* at that script! "

So before you let them loose on the business, make it clear to the vendor: the end-user doesn't care how the tiny bits of the system are built – she just wants it to deliver on the spec. Assure them that the user believes they know their stuff – she doesn't need living proof – and she is very definitely not as excited as the supplier is about precisely how this is done...

Language is very important in this situation, too. Ask the supplier to avoid slipping into Vulcan. I have seen a supplier delightedly announce that he would be inventing some new jargon solely for this Programme. He proposed a new language that everyone on the Programme could share so that we would all be talking about the same thing. I said no thanks (more politely than the idea deserved) but instead we could just use the terms people in our business already used for the various transactions that were under development.

Explain to suppliers that you are doing your best to engage end-users in their business. The more familiar the new stuff sounds, the better the chances of engaging people and achieving rapid adoption of the new ideas, kit and techniques. Ask them not to put barriers in the way. And then let them go and do their thing.

Always give an opportunity for the business to meet the suppliers. Keeping them at arm's length is both unfair and unproductive.

3.   It's ours, not mine

This also applies to both parties. The vendor may bring a unique widget or process; but it will doubtlessly be more effective if the client is allowed to adapt it slightly to suit the precise needs of end-users. Vendors shouldn't be precious about this. Instead, they should think of it as someone helping them with their long-term product development.

This idea broadens out to all the IP involved in the programme. Vendors who are new to collaborative partnership will often still be shaking off the old paradigm of Never Give Anything Away. So they operate Phoney Partnership Working – the bit where they simply harvest the client's ideas. They squirrel these away for use with their next client, but they give nothing back in exchange.

When the buyer spots this is happening, he immediately hugs his IP very close to his chest. Now neither of us are giving anything away. No partnership is occurring. The solution is not blossoming.

Consequently, you need to create an environment where the supplier is comfortable sharing. Emphasize that they'll be amazed at what you might be able to add to their widget or process, making it a much chunkier thing they can sell elsewhere. Explain that both parties are growing their IP. You, of course, are growing your IP ahead of the rest of your sector, so it doesn't matter if the supplier goes on and sells it to your competitors – you're still ahead of the game.

4. It's us, not them

Both the above points have led me to conclude that it's almost impossible for most parts of a programme to be successfully developed in a hand-me-down format. The client-team acting as intermediaries between the wider transformation team and the suppliers *guarantees* loss of relevance, content, ownership and innovative thinking.

Instead, I firmly believe that hybrid teams combining client and vendor members will always work best. Decision-making will be improved by having a wider breadth of knowledge and experience; and differing perspectives. Contextual understanding will be improved by having insiders present, avoiding unworkable flights of fancy. And the combined ideas will always be bigger than the ideas each side would have had on its own.

Working collaboratively like this reduces the tendency towards blame in favour of shared goals and joint responsibility. Yet again, more focus is placed on getting it right rather than in holding forensic investigations into who got it wrong.

5. Warts and all disclosure

When leading a programme, I don't *ever* want to be simply told that everything's fine. I want to be told precisely how it's fine, or less than fine, or a that it's a rare old catastrophe. And yet vendors who are not working in true partnership will often persist with the old-school assumption that it's essential to appear swan-like, cool and unruffled by anything the buyer raises. Vendors using this out-dated approach will give a firm one-sentence reassurance that what is being requested can be done/is in hand/has been fixed; and then not elaborate further.

The trouble is, no-one is reassured by an unsubstantiated reassurance. It is assumed that no swan-like behaviour is occurring back at Vendor HQ – more likely, it's headless-chicken-central. The customer does not need reassurance: he/she needs transparency. In true partnership working the problem is defined and shared. Indeed, we might *all* be part of the solution.

Create an atmosphere in which the vendors are not in fear for their lives if they hit a snag. Allow them to be honest when they find a problem – indeed, actively and vigorously encourage honesty, because they may not be used to this being OK. You're looking for vendors who have the courage to tell us there are problems – alongside telling us what they are doing to fix them, of course. They need to know that you'll help with the solution where appropriate.

Silence is not golden; it's suspicious.

6. Is it a solve or a sell?

Vendors who are truly working in partnership will have the client's best interests at heart. They will want to come out of the Programme with another sale; or a glowing recommendation, referral or review. Consequently, because they value their brand, they will not mis-sell or mislead you: it wouldn't be in their interests to do so.

Therefore, always be initially open-minded to any recommendations for further products or services that they suggest – they may well be solving problems, rather than just selling you stuff you don't need. Don't assume they're trying to fleece you when they may be just thinking smarter.

It's extremely easy to identify whether you need this proposed add-on or not. You just ask: "does this item contribute to delivering the Minimal Viable Product on time – or does it exceed it?" Anything that over-delivers, you don't need. Which is why, what you really, really have to have crystal clear is…

7. *Governance, governance, governance*

Partnership working is often taken to mean there will be the muddiest of waters if something goes wrong. Buyer-organisations tend to think it's best that everyone has a distinct place in the pecking order so that someone can be taken out and shot if needed.

Instead, I'd argue that:

a) First off, partnership working reduces the need for firing squads, because there are *fewer unsolved problems*. Partners first disclose and then fix problems, rather than these becoming nasty surprises uncovered at crisis point.

b) There needs never be any fudge over who's responsible for what. Responsibilities and obligations can be agreed ahead in a businesslike manner. I once drew up a partner's responsibilities for an extremely complicated transformation on 1.5 sides of A4.

You can also cover any worries about IP dissemination here but bear in mind you'll be first-to-market with anything you jointly invent, which is what really matters.

c) The secret is to keep a tight rein on checking that we're *all* delivering against the expectation. So a weekly governance meeting that objectively holds to account all parties on progress against their obligations is essential. Putting governance in the hands of a programme sponsor who isn't a deliverer is key. (See Governance, Chapter 9).

When it's time to say goodbye

Just occasionally, you will be forced to admit that it's really not working out and that you have no future together. If you've followed guidance on partnership-model supplier relationships, then this sad moment won't occur very often. However, it's not unknown, especially in situations where you might have a, er, heritage supplier, one you've inherited. What do you do?

- **Avoid it if you can**. Smart contracting is critical and will minimise it occurring. This includes contracts in which both parties are given the option to terminate the agreement.

- **Recognise we're in a bad place.** No-one likes to be wrong. But if you selected the wrong provider, or they've delivered less than you thought they would, then quickly admit it – especially to yourself. Papering over the cracks won't help.

- **Point out that there's an elephant in the room**. A really quite large one, which is lumbering about angrily and breaking all the furniture. When everyone knows it isn't working, you have to say so, and start a discussion about where we are now. There is still time to save the day.

  Tell the supplier frankly how frustrated and disappointed you are. Then shut up. Let them tell you how they will fix it.

I've found that the situation can sometimes be plucked from the jaws of defeat if you keep the supplier but change the humans. A new Account Director or Dev Lead might well turn it around. Try to re-engineer the day-to-day relationship if you think that people are the problem.

As a first port of call, you might try offering help to get them back on track – such as by changing how your team interacts with theirs. It may be a six-and-two-threes situation.

This may be enough: but if not….

- **Recognise the point of no return**. I've found that typically this moment comes when *you* believe the supplier is not delivering what you want or expect; and yet *they* genuinely believe that they are. They are refusing to put up the white flag or offer reparations. That's the point of no return.

  So if you are not seeing continuous progress, but stalling or reversing; or there is repeated failure to deliver against milestones; or a regular lack of quality – then it's Thank You and Goodnight.

- **Generate some options**. Ask contract management team to give you options for exit. Don't be afraid to call it with these colleagues – even though you might look like you failed.

In transformation, I think more energy is wasted on under-performing suppliers than anything else. Be decisive and don't give it too long – contract-waving, post-mortems and finger-pointing will eat energy like nothing else. Decree Nisi time.

In Case of Emergency, Break Glass

Pyramid sellers

Many transformation programmes – even quite modest affairs – will have multiple suppliers. It is common for supplier management to become a massively time-consuming task. This happens particularly when there's some old-school behaviour raising its ugly head – such as responsibility-ducking, deadline-blindness or finger-pointing.

Ideally, this can be mitigated at the start of the programme, but in an emergency, vendor vendettas can be fixed by simply restructuring the chain of command. So, instead of all suppliers having equal status, and equal calls on your team's time, you arrange them in a pyramid format. You make one supplier the prime player, responsible for the delivery of all the others. Then, the prime supplier becomes responsible to you for getting work out of the door and dispute de-fusing – and you don't have to. You now have just one point of contact for contract delivery.

"Yes, but", I hear you holler, "That'll come with a price tag. The prime supplier will want to be rewarded for the risk and effort they are taking."

"Yes, but", I reply, "The only other option is to find the budget for in-house resource to police the squabbles." It costs the same either way, but there is every chance there is greater capability for the role within a large and experienced supplier company than inside your team.

173

12. Walking them up the aisle

Engaging the business

And here we are. We've finally arrived at the Really Big Deal. For me, engaging the business is the most important part of digital transformation.

Your Programme will not be considered a success unless its content makes a difference to the business. It will not make a difference unless it is adopted by the users. The users will not adopt it unless they believe there's something in it for them; that it's an improvement on what went before; and that it's worth the effort of changing their actions and behaviour for. Consequently, you will need to persuade all users that this change is *worth it*.

For me, engagement always has two key features:

- A good sell-in, creating an appetite with good communication of the benefits of change
- A good and credible solution that satisfies the appetite created.

If you don't have both, you don't get engagement. If you don't get engagement, you don't get transformation. But "engagement" is, in my view, a bit of a lightweight relationship. I don't want them engaged – I want them *married* to the idea. So that we can hustle them along to the Register Office before they change their minds. Where do you start?

Game face

Start with yourself. You will need to present the right disposition throughout the programme, and particularly when dealing with C-Suite colleagues. You will need them to trust and respect you, and for that some suggested principles and techniques are:

- **Balancing act.** You'll need a balance between not too pushy and not too subservient. Yes, I know, IT was pushed around by other C-Suite members in the 80s and 90s, but this is no time to try our hands at yelling as loud as they did. We need to lead in the modern way, persuasively and engagingly. But equally, we shouldn't be too subservient: we may be the new boys and girls, but we're not there to serve as Marketing's research team or Ops' technicians.

- **Voice of reason.** Don't be tempted to make a grand entrance, such as by making a big splash with the trendiest technology or half-tested innovation. It won't do you any favours if you get a reputation for chasing rainbows. But equally, you don't want to be the person with a problem for every solution. You're aiming for calm, reasonable and constructive positivity.

- **Revenge is a dish best put in the bin.** There's a digital transformation Programme. Our job is to deliver it. End of. But often, when people have been denied power for a long time, they've spent many years plotting what they will do, come the revolution. You will naturally have long-held ideas about how things should be done. And yet now is not necessarily the time to take our revenge on that only-listen-to-Marketing 1990s leadership by implementing our highly-prized-pet-project, which has been simmering quietly since the Stone Roses first went a bit quiet. Unless it delivers the Programme, its moment has passed!

- **Have the courage of your concoctions.** Finally and most importantly, even though you don't want to tread on any toes or trash any relationships, keep in mind that you and your team really do know more about this digital business than everyone else around the table. If you have an innovation that the business really needs, make your very best case for it and if that doesn't work first time, try at least once more!

These characteristics will earn the respect of your senior colleagues. However, this is not just a show you put on for high days and holidays. You will need to demonstrate this same calm, positive and reasonable demeanour in your interactions with everyone in the organisation. That's all day, every day.

Why? Because your team's culture comes from the top. They will begin to behave in calm, reasonable and positive ways if that's what they see you doing. That's the culture you will need for a successful Programme. And of course, if you have a couple of rogues for whom calm, reasonable and positive doesn't come naturally, you will be perfectly placed to ask them to change their behaviour, having led by example.

VIP Treatment

Having reinvented yourself as The Official Voice of Reason, the next step is to engage the top team. If the leadership team is onside with a) you and b) your Programme, life will run a little easier. Note: this is not grovelling, smarming or flannelling. The top team tends to be very astute and will see through all that nonsense immediately. Instead, it's a programme of activity designed to build their trust and actively demonstrate the benefits of your digital transformation.

Let me give you an example from history…

About a hundred years ago, I did my first transformation and innovation gig. We'd got to the stage where we knew what needed to be done, with all the movers-and-doers agreed on what the scope was and even what the route was. Then someone heard a rumour that the Top Floor was getting a bit antsy, having seen the cost projections.

My job was to go up and talk them round. As I was only a bairn, then, I tried to put off the evil moment with a spot of research. Not financial, market or tech research: no, it was nosing into what the bosses were thinking. By leaning chattily on the desk of a PA for 20 minutes, I found out that most of the resistance was due to lack of knowledge – these folks just didn't get why the changes we were proposing would be useful.

I asked the stores' manager to give me a Blackberry. For any reader under 25, a Blackberry was the prototype smartphone of its day, a device for which you needed the fingers of a four-year-old, which reached the height of its popularity in the Tottenham Riots in 2011 (don't ask). At the time of our story, it was bleeding-edge technology.

I got the Blackberry rigged up so that the key opinion-leader could use it to watch the stock exchange do its stuff. I took it up to him and showed him how to work it. Naturally, he was like a kid on Christmas morning: and the budget sailed through the next week.

That was not a spurious exercise in manipulating people with Boys' Toys. It was a living demonstration of why technology was worth its cost to the business. You will need to be alert to all opportunities to prove the cost/benefit of your Programme with brief and impactful real-life examples.

In many organisations, it's worth making enormous efforts to engage the top team, for exactly the reasons just described. Remember, the Exec Team genuinely *is* different from the rest of the organisation, so something bespoke is not just indulging them – it's a true necessity.

I suggest the following five considerations:

1)   They do unique jobs

The Exec Team really doesn't do the same stuff as everyone else. They will each have a unique role within the business. So it's never wise to give them the same kit as everyone else: common sense. For a start, the senior team will include plenty of Road Warriors, never at the same desk for more than a couple of days, obliged to haul their IT kit around in Louis Vuitton, visiting bits of the world that might have only just heard of broadband. These people spend more time at conferences than they do in coffee shops. They're interested in moment-by-moment share prices and Libor rates and sterling vs the Colombian Peso.

Nominate a bright and personable member of your team to walk round in their heads for a bit, mentally wearing pinstripe and making notes with a Mont Blanc. He/she needs to get a handle on what they do and what's important to them, person by person. Then give each one solutions that precisely fit his/her concerns – if it's the lightest-weight laptop; or a dedicated conference set-up team; or a personalised exchange-rate screen, it'll be a worthwhile investment.

2)   *Their time really is precious*

Leadership Team time is the most expensive person-hour in the whole business: and therefore, their downtime is the organisation's most expensive downtime. Every second wasted is worth big bucks. So we have to make their time pay. Rule 1 is always: no learning curve. These people are too expensive to have them spending time learning how to use the new technology. Instead, you have to source or adapt technology so that they'll get it, right away. You put the hours in so they don't have to. By the way, this has the added benefit of them really rating you for doing that....

Rule 2 is to anticipate where time might get wasted. For example, we don't want them unable to get online or on the phone when they go to the new acquisition in Outer Darkest Furthermost Nether Region. So it's a good idea to have access to their calendar a year out; spot the visits where this kind of problem will occur; and rock up in their office two weeks before the trip with a phone that works just like theirs except that it's tuned for the local network.

3)   You cannot always get direct access

Senior executives do not tend to operate open door policies or welcome techies wandering in to, like, er, fix the router, mate. They are busy and often inaccessible. Therefore, remember Rule 3: the PA is your friend.

The secret to the relationship with the Exec is gaining the PA's trust first. The PA controls access to the Exec, is the Gatekeeper of the Sacred Diary and knows what makes this Exec tick. You need a positive relationship with this very senior member of the team, because if the PA goes into Rottweiler mode, you're lost. So see what your box of tricks has in it to make the PA's life easier; respect the importance of the PA role; and lean on the desk and chat a bit to find out what you can do to win over this particular C-suiter.

4)   Five-star service works

You'll need to deliver five-star service. That's not because
Senior Execs expect no less: it's because that's how you'll get
the job done to best effect.

Perhaps you're going to need an IT Butler per Exec. And
therefore, in larger organisations, probably a team of IT
Butlers and Valets. Because the IT Butlers are the techies who
will make everything OK – and do it with charm and calm.
Even at 2am, with the Exec in Sydney who can't access his
Cloud. You'll need techies who are great fixers, but more
importantly have exceptional customer service skills, who can
hold a conversation while they work and who inspire
confidence, even under extreme pressure dealing with
occasionally strung-out, pressured people.   Recruit them
wisely.

5)   It's in your best interests

For me, it's extremely important to take care of the Exec team
for all the reasons given above. But there's another reason.
The bottom line is that it's the Leadership Team members who
sign off and then sponsor any transformation programme.
And if the Execs think what you're doing is not clever or fit for
purpose, you can wave goodbye to your sponsorship or
funding. So you always need to make sure your top team is …
how shall I put it? … properly taken care of.

Another job for the A Team

Next, get yourself professional help. You may well have a GCSE in English and a pen, but this doesn't make you a professional communicator. Yes, I know, you communicate all day, every day, but that doesn't mean you can craft and deliver a nuanced communications strategy. Blimey, you don't think I wrote this book all by myself, do you?

I've mentioned the skills and qualities you're looking for above (*The A team*, Chapter 10), and that implies you'll need to create a full-time role. That's true if you're running a very large and fast Programme, but not necessarily so for a less ambitious affair. You might consider hiring a consultant for a couple of days a month; or there may even be talent in Marketing, PR or Internal Communications you could borrow.

The point is, engagement will be achieved as part of a structured and staged communication programme, and you will need guidance on moving through the steps. Basically, these are as follows….

Wooing, Courting and Engagement

You next need to work on engaging the wider business – and even some people outside the business - throughout your programme. The stages are:

1)   Create an appetite with the vision

This is more wowing than wooing.

We all know that people don't like their IT going all different. In fact, they have a habit of passionately loathing IT change and the time it takes to learn about new tools and methods. So transformation always has to sell itself hard, from the very start.

Very early in the project, it's important to communicate visibly on the Wow Factor. This involves stating your vision and then bringing it to life. Instead of *talking* about the new system, **show** people a few sexy new functions and some mouth-watering capabilities. They will immediately see the benefits it would bring and many will become excited and enthusiastic about adopting it. Instead of resisting, some of them will be banging on the door wanting to know how soon you can get the new stuff on their desks. These people are engaged. You've started.

Of course, there's always a lengthy time gap between whetting the organisation's appetite for the new system – and actually delivering it. It's easy for people to become cynical and decide in a seen-it-all-before way that it's never going to happen.

To minimise loss of appetite, make a plan for showing the various parts of the business the relevant parts of the system as it evolves. This can keep them keen. I believe the key to keeping appetite sharp is regular interesting communication and delivering on promises. It's therefore not difficult.

2)   *Use Discovery for engagement*

Discovery is about finding things out. But used intelligently, it's also the first step in engaging people across the business.

Consulting widely with people from all parts of the business won't necessarily mean you get 200 conflicting views. I'm often surprised by how much synergy there is in requirements across the board, in fact. What you will definitely get, though, are 200 people who feel they had their say. As such, they feel a little bit important and have a sense that this Programme is about what *they* want. They had a chance to make suggestions for improvements and they've been truly-madly-deeply listened to.

Again, your Discovery Team needs to be briefed that 50% of their role in this exercise is engaging and stimulating their colleagues. They absolutely should not be telling people what we can't do; why that'll never work; and how we tried it in 1991 and it didn't work then, either.

Your Discovery Team should also use their interactions with the Divisions/Departments to identify humans who, well, *get it*. People who demonstrate enthusiasm for a new way of doing things can be co-opted as peripatetic Programme team members. Here's how:

3)   *Use development for engagement*

There's more below on the types of development you might pursue to deliver your programme. However, one of the major advantages of using an agile development model is the opportunity to involve end-users in the development process. Where possible, I'd sit representatives of the Division or Department right at the heart of developing the new stuff. They can work within the development team for some of the time, informing the process as it builds, so that what they get is exactly what they want.

Of course, that's time away from their desk and the day job. For that, you'll need permission from a leadership team which is well-wedded to the Programme. See above on that score....

Your honorary development team members will ultimately become your best advocates for selling-in the solutions once they get back to their own teams. They become the Programme's on-the-ground Champions and Ambassadors. The message, coming from them and not the Programme Team, is often more credible and persuasive.

4)   *Communicate honestly, clearly and with purpose*

Throughout the programme, you will need to keep positive messages coming in order to persuade the business that a) this is definitely happening, so get ready; and b) it will be A Good Thing. If the Programme goes quiet, it falls into disrepute.

You will need a recognised communication structure, so that people know: (1) where to go to get information; and (2) when it's important to listen-up.

Within your chosen communication structure, it's always best to deliver the same information using multiple channels. This reduces the chance of a gem being missed; and it also allows for curious the fact that Not All People Are The Same. I suggest putting out the most important messages in multiple ways, to suit all preferences for communication – e.g. with pictures, with voice and with writing.

All messages need to be clearly explained using language you are certain the listeners/readers will understand. Keep off the jargon unless you're talking to people who speak your language.

My three golden rules for communication are: **honesty** (the truth about the matter); **clarity** (easily understood language and content); and **purpose** (why we're doing this). And of course, it takes a lot of silent listening to understand what to say to get this part spot-on.

5)   *Tailor the communication*

Never use a one-size-fits-all message. Yes, I know: this approach appears to take more time/effort/resource/pratting about, because you have to devise tailored messages for all types of audience – right down to small groups or even influential single individuals. But for me, it's a resource well-spent, because tailored-communication means people understand and buy-in quicker, better, faster, more. The personalised message is always real and relevant to the listener/reader. You decide what's in your message simply by listening quietly to what the audience currently thinks.

6)   *Use testing for engagement*

Testing can and should be a real crowd-pleaser. I'd recommend extending testing beyond your "champions" and "ambassadors", described above – they're already in the tent. I'd recruit testers from other parts of the relevant Division or Department, so that even more socks are blown off. Of course, if you're developing in an agile format, this cohort can be with you for some time, but if it's traditional UAT, tweaking things a bit at the end, I'd select the Departmental Refuseniks to be the testers.

And no apologies for repeating that the testing team needs to be briefed that their role is persuasive. They need to be very clear that the testers are helping, not criticising, and that there is no place for defensiveness and "Ah, but what you don't realise is…" elitism. It would be a good idea for the testers to get some tips from the trainers – always assuming these are different humans.

7)   *Use training for engagement*

Use talented trainers! I know the developers are the experts – but it doesn't always make them the best people to talk empathetically and persuasively to the uninitiated.

Here's an astonishing fact. Even though you've shouted about your Programme for months or years, communicating weekly to the business, there will still be plenty of users who walk into the training session having not given the transformation one second's thought until that moment. They will potentially start to hear, for the very first time, what an enormously Big Deal this is going to be in their life. Fear will potentially make them angry, unco-operative or just sulky-fourth-former disengaged.

They will need empathy, time and attention in order to bring them round. So hand-pick the very best trainers. I find that people who are natural teachers are more useful than people who know all there is to know about the system: they can always ask an expert if there's a tough question.

And resource it well: if you can't run to a full-on training team, I'd recommend a cascade system that trains-up Power Users who are then embedded in each Department. My preferred ratio is one Power User to four other staff members. This close-knit team, with its trusted and embedded expertise, ensures everyone has knowledge and information handy-by, in their language and relevant to their needs.

8)   *Measure engagement*

You need to monitor whether or not you are bringing most people along through the whole experience. As everyone knows, significant change of any kind can be a challenging and often even a threatening experience. And most people don't react well to being threatened…

Pay attention to the relationship between digital change and cultural change. Your Programme will inevitably force cultural and behavioural change on just about everyone in the organisation. And conversely, perhaps cultural change will be needed if the new ways of working are to be wholeheartedly adopted. This means you always need a handle on where the organisation is in its relationship with your Programme.

Therefore, you'll regularly need to know the answer to a very wassocky question: "How is everyone feeling about the programme today?". No, this is not something from *West One*, but a serious mindset you'll need to adopt. You'll need a constantly-updated barometer of opinion, to check that we're largely keeping the business on the bus. This topic is so important that it's a candidate for one of the traffic lights you'll need to devise for your governance meetings.

That should take you through to launch. But then comes a different set of responsibilities: ensuring continued use of the newly-transformed technology and processes. If all the previous communications were carrots, it's now necessary to have a stick, too, just in case...

I'd recommend that everyone in the organisation is given an "adoption KPI" they need to meet. This might involve, for example, attendance at training and achieving a targeted level of performance. You might go so far as to include proper competence exams, and pass marks and certificates and everything.

Yes, you will need the agreement of the C-Suite to include this in everyone's annual performance review and personal objectives. In some organisations, it may even carry punishments (e.g. bonus target not met = computer says no). So it may be a very big stick indeed. But it does measure - and drive – engagement. And by heck, it doesn't half make the new IT system really matter. Especially to those people who otherwise would have preferred not to bother...

In Case of Emergency, Break Glass

Breakfast Menu

If you're struggling to get people in the organisation engaged, remember that Peter Drucker said, "Culture eats strategy for breakfast". Use a breakfast-based method to make your transformation strategy look as tempting and familiar as bacon, sausage and scrambled eggs. Here are three simple courses. I mean, ideas:

Point out it isn't avocado on toast. Where people are very resistant to change, it can be effective if your transformation appears to be an awful lot like what went before. User experience is key. If the user experience – the screen, the archiving mechanism, the functionality – is still familiar (if a bit smoother, cleaner or faster), it'll still look like beans and fried bread and not some trendy non-breakfast that is only ever served within sight of the Sydney Opera House. Effort put into creating surface familiarity will get reluctant users over their initial scepticism.

Tell them it IS avo on toast. Where things are *really* broken and the audience is hungry for change, then be bold and tell the audience that the transformation will bring them a completely new experience. The old-fashioned content will be left behind. Even highly-resistant people can be wowed by getting rid of frustrating old kit and processes. Paradoxically, this type of message can be used in tandem with (1) – people really can believe two different things at the same time!

Agree that it IS avocado on toast, but let them find out it tastes like bacon... Some audience segments will remain suspicious, even if they really want the new benefits the transformation will bring. This is where you definitely need to move from *describing* the freshness of the healthy, luscious, ripe avocado – and let them *taste* it for themselves. Trial – long before the UAT stage – will win a good percentage of acceptance. It takes away the fear of change that comes from not truly thinking about the nature of the change. The new system isn't that scary after all...

OK: now you're thinking that honesty thing I mentioned earlier has gone right out of the Little Chef window.   I'm telling everyone what they want to hear and I'll soon come a cropper.

I'd argue that's not the case. A successful communication plan does not treat the workforce as a single homogenous audience, but instead takes time and effort to address the huge variety of viewpoints that stakeholders will have. Yes, that means you will need different messages for different audience segments. As long as those messages are factually based and provable, they will *all* be honest and credible.

We now live in a world where it is relatively easy to tailor communications to smaller interest-groups: the trick is simply to have a communications strategy that puts in the hard yards and makes the effort to create targeted messaging.

13. Time is of the essence

Transforming fast

If you want the best return on your investment, you need to transform quickly. You'll see the business benefits soonest. Obviously, however, it's also necessary for the credibility of your transformation that it's (largely) *right*, as well. So there's a balance to be struck between speed and perfection. In my career, I've run one Programme that converted oodles of sites on five continents in 22 months: and others that took five years or longer.

So, how do you strike that balance?

Anything is possible

A quick response is always possible. We all proved that in 2020 when the Covid-19 pandemic hit all countries of the world and new processes such as remote working had to be introduced almost overnight. There was no choice. But I'd argue that a quick response is *always* possible, and that availability of choice has nothing to do with it.

In one of my roles, I was tasked with deployment on what was then the fastest and largest ever separation in the food industry. In 22 months, we set the business up as an independent producer, working on all continents.

Achieving that deadline was due to hard graft and taking one significant decision: to use out-of-the-box solutions, with little to no customisation. We set up the new organisation with new processes, as per the off-the-shelf technology, balanced with a clear focus on customer requirements. It can be done.

How to set the Speed Dial

Yes, it can be done – but is it right to do it? I'd suggest there is one consideration that will tell you how quickly you need to go. The customers.

The customer needs to be central. We need accurate information, constantly updated, on what the customers are thinking. And the transformation activity needs to be buzzing around these views and needs, working very quickly and nimbly if customer needs and expectations change.

High speed. The Programme described above was entirely in response to customer expectations. They wanted a provider whose systems would jigsaw-puzzle-piece lock onto their own, with no loss of service as the company's ownership transitioned. It was the only way the new company would keep the old company's clients.

And because that organisation was going through such a seismic change, the workforce recognised the magnitude of the demerger and therefore expected and largely accepted very significant changes to everything they did and how they did it. That kind of speed is an option for when the situation is ... drastic.

That's very tough to do at speed unless everyone the organisation is clear about the external driver of the change – for example, that we're in a "change or die" scenario. In these circumstances, your communication must be beyond excellent. See previous chapter.

Variable speed. Not every digital change is responding to something drastic within or around the business, but nonetheless, the customer still needs to be the central point of focus. Common sense.

You'll need to offer a rapid response to the customers' ever-changing needs. And needs change all the time: for example, people in Leeds didn't know they needed digital bus stops to tell them precisely when the next bus would arrive, until Transport for London showed them how handy it could be….

So be prepared to bring forward parts of your Programme that are customer facing whenever the need becomes apparent.

Steady speed. In less extreme circumstances, I'd advise that change – especially when affecting people and processes - has one essential sister-principle: you must win hearts and minds. If your customers are not urgently demanding change, you can take a *little bit* more time to bring the organisation along on the journey – always assuming the CFO will let you spend money with no sign of an immediate ROI...

And as I'll explore further in Chapter 15 (*Mission Crop*), if *any* of your competitors are upping their offer, it's time to put the pedal to the metal.

Waterfall or Agile?

The debate rages on. Do you use waterfall or agile for digital transformation? Which will afford you the greatest speed?

Well, it depends.

What a cop out, I hear you howl. No, let me explain. It depends on what else you want to achieve as well as speed. That's because, done properly, both methods can give you rapid progress. Or what about a compromise...?

Waterfall – the pros and cons

Here, the supplier sits outside the business and produces phased development that takes weeks or months, to your agreed deadline. If you can afford to resource this fully, the timescales can be very short, as the developer can put huge resources into the project. See what you can do in 22 months, above.

Waterfall has the additional benefit for the Programme Lead of making all the problems go away, using specialists and saving the business resources. Typically, offshore companies carry out your development for a fraction of the cost of shopping local.

But there can be problems:

- It's very easy to fall into the mindset of "marking the supplier's homework". It can be difficult to develop a true partnership, rather than the old-fashioned type of supplier relationship.

- Long-distance supervision can be difficult to achieve in practical terms, and you can suddenly find yourself with problems that no-one warned you about. Personally, I prefer to have better oversight.

- It's also easy to keep that supplier at one remove from the business. They don't get a chance to pick up all the ideas and minor requirements that come from working closely with the people who'll use the system.

- I tend to feel concerned that, with the waterfall model, if it goes wrong, then more than a heavy weight of water will come crashing down on your head. It can make very rapid progress in the wrong direction very quickly, however good your oversight.

Given a free choice I'd confine waterfall delivery to picturesque becks and babbling brook – i.e. using it occasionally, for minor pieces of work, with trusted suppliers.

Agile – for and against

For Programmes that aren't up against the clock and resourced with budgets to meet a demanding deadline, I'd recommend agile. My main arguments in its favour would be:

The business sees it all happening. You can check back in with your stakeholders every fortnight, giving them something new to chew on, test and examine. They will be highly-engaged in the evolving solution – and they'll see tangible progress as you head for the finish line.

It builds stakeholders' confidence. Stakeholders see what's happened in the project and know what is going to happen next. They understand the hurdles you're clambering over and any tricky problems get on their radar early, so come as less of a shock. They also see a lot of problems solved within each fortnight, giving them further reassurance that it's all going to be OK.

The stakeholders can't send it off track. People often worry that agile delivery allows the stakeholders too much influence on the project. First I'd say, hey, these people are the internal customers, and we all know what the customer never is. They must be allowed to describe what they want and judge whether our efforts meet that need. But second, more pragmatically, you can mitigate any risk of mission-creep by using skilled business analysts, who translate between the business and the developers and who are drilled to Stay Focused On What's Important at all times.

The business benefits from being involved. Agile is well-known for making a lot of demands on the business, asking stakeholders to commit vast amounts of time to development solutions. And yes, you will undoubtedly have to ask for a lot of their time. But instead of resenting that, the business tends to see the benefits – they're getting what they really want; they're seeing opportunities to develop the organisation and streamline processes as they go; they understand the system and how it could be further evolved in future; sometimes they even believe their IT is going to be a growth-enabler. Heaven forfend!

It can keep going. In truly agile delivery, your changes can be in a state of permanently-continuing. It always gets better.

However...

Agile is easily misunderstood by the business. Because this type of development involves the business in seeing your workings-out, it can be misinterpreted and then can develop a reputation for being a solution made on the hoof.   You will need really good communications to explain that we are not "making it up as we go along" or "launching before it's ready" or "getting the business to solve all the problems".

Hybrid – or how to compromise
So what's the compromise? How about a hybrid programme that uses both agile and waterfall. Not a fudge, just pragmatic common sense. I've used hybrid with some success, especially with near-shore development providers, where the practical supplier-management challenges reduce.

Nearshore hybrid lives inside the business and is far more likely to offer a suitable development solution at speed. You can still use large development teams – I've used teams of 50 or 60 people each containing a blend of in-house people, contractors and near-shore developers.

The advantages are:

R.E.S.P.E.C.T. First up, this methodology builds a level of trust and respect akin to that found in a hippie commune. You will leverage the developers' expertise and their knowledge will help the in-house team members spark-up their ideas. Working closely together puts everyone on the same side.

Eye to eye contact. For me, communication's the bottom-line, driving force, crucial factor in innovation programmes. It can work particularly using near-shore development resource, for three reasons:

First, you'll have the team members talking to each other all the time. Everyone can have close contact, with daily conversations throughout their working day, which runs at much the same time as our own. By making good use of unified communications widgets and gadgets it doesn't cost much money either. It's probably simply the amount and frequency of conversation and interaction that makes the near-shore team and the in-house team feel genuinely part of the whole Programme team.

Next, I suggest mixing it up and then joining it up. Set your in-house people to lead the development teams. Therefore, each team comprises Us and Them, but we're all on the same side. It works, because both teams work roughly the same hours and stuff gets done in real-time. As a result, you'll see close collaboration and genuine responsibility-sharing partnering.

And third, it's also easy to go there. That means there's more face to face discussion and we're building real relationships. Although in some European regions, this approach is not suitable for vegetarians….

You're at the wheel. Finally, with near-shore hybrid, you're driving, but we can still keep an eye on the kids in the back.

The amount and quality of communication makes it easier to retain leadership and management of the programme, even when the developers have taken something away to work on. You know what's going on; the supplier will be unavoidably and immediately honest if they hit a snag; and you see quite clearly that they are listening and following your directions.

What's the risk? The biggest risk is that everyone gets carried away! You will need very clear objectives based on the needs of the business, and governance that keeps the excitement in check, with a close eye on the MVP.

In Case of Emergency, Break Glass

End of the Beginning

One problem occurs quite often when a transformation is working against the clock: failure to solidify the MVP. Typically, what happens is that deadlines are so tight, you will be working on developing and delivering simultaneously with identifying your MVP. You're in learning-by-doing mode. You're identifying what you *can* do whilst still not having identified what you *should* do.

This will cause the purpose and the output of the Programme to be poorly defined – which invariably results in an expensive free-for-all, with he-who-shouts-loudest being the only satisfied customer.

Stop. Draw a breath. *Choose* to make identification of the MVP a priority.

Set a date by which you will agree the MVP – or at least, the headline content of the MVP. This date marks the end of the beginning. Discussion of "potential" output is replaced on this day with discussion of "planned" output. We are committed.

This method has a very interesting side-effect. It drives engagement.

That's because those people who want to have their area of operation included in the transformation suddenly recognise they need to get involved. Instead of telling you they're too busy to talk to you until at least the middle of next April, they will find time to ensure you are aware of their requirements before the MVP is agreed ... on MVPD-Day.

14.Change their minds

Running the team

Amazon, Waterstones and your local independent bookshop have plenty of other books about how to lead a team. Many acres of print are devoted to setting objectives, steering, empowering, motivating and measuring teams. That wheel does not need reinvention.

Therefore, I'm keeping it brief in this chapter and confining myself to points that are specific to running a *digital transformation* team. In our discipline, we face some issues which are possibly unique to IT-based teams, so I'm going to address just those. I've mentioned above about hiring the right people for the job, but you don't always get to cherry pick your A-Team. This chapter deals with some of our unique issues in IT.

Cultural revolution

One of the biggest leadership issues for projects with IT at their core is the culture of any existing team. It will often be necessary to shift the existing kept-in-the-box-until-needed culture that a team has become used to. When you think about culture change, it always seems a bit, well, MASSIVE. It's knowing where to start. But in fact, sometimes it needs no more than a sharp tug on a piece of string....

Years ago, I started on a programme where the client told us that IT was hindering rather than helping the organisation. Systems were complicated, the technology was something of a Dark Art and the IT team was remote and unhelpful.

I immediately went off to find this allegedly-rogue IT team to get their side of the story. After a couple of hours, I tracked them down on the eighth floor, in a small glass walled office with the blinds closed. I opened the door, gave a sharp tug on a piece of string … and opened the blinds. The cultural revolution had begun…

This is my favourite story to illustrate the status of IT in many organisations in the past – teams would be marginalised and commoditised by the business and they had quite naturally responded by hiding themselves away. You will need a very much more upfront and out-there team if your transformation is to be a success. Start by opening the blinds and letting the world see IT, then shift the team from blinking in the bright light to fully match fit.

Silence, please: transformation communication in progress

Over the years, it's dawned on me that the majority of communication is NOT about broadcasting. When I'm working on bringing an existing team on side, my golden rule is: *listen – first and last and always.*

Earlier, I proudly pointed out my astute observation that I am neither perfect nor psychic. Therefore, I do not have all the answers and I do not know all the facts. Consequently, the only way I can arrive at answers is to obtain facts and ideas from other people. I have to understand what other people believe and what they know.

I would strongly recommend that all transformation leads improve their listening skills. You can never be good enough at listening. So at the start of a transformation programme, I 'd recommend sitting down with all the people in your team specifically with the purpose of listening to what they know and think. You can then collect together honest and un-interpreted views; and where necessary, put together groups to develop the thinking further.   Asked and listen to the team – just as you would when you were questioning the business to create a true problem statement.

Then, you have to keep on making opportunities for listening. For example, in the past we've developed cross-over teams comprised of in-house people and external developers to make sure we're all ears-wide-open; and we've listened as open-mindedly to colleagues as we have to UAT testers.

That level of listening builds both relationships and your credibility as a leader. It means that team members are engaged, knowledge is maximised and everyone feels their contribution is valued. This could be a very new experience for some IT teams!

Change the behaviour, not the password

Here's another anecdote – I'm in Jackanory mode today. I have an example I use to illustrate the importance of security on any Programme. I ask the team: "If a person near to you on the train is using a laptop, will you compulsively want to have a look at what he/she has on her screen? Please answer yes or no."

I don't mind what they answer, I just want them to think about it. Because those people who are not remotely interested in what another businessperson is doing are potentially at a high degree of security risk. They wouldn't dream of nosey-parkering about someone else's work – they're too busy, not interested, or too polite. Therefore, they assume (if only subconsciously) that no-one would do that to them. Wrong.

A good percentage of team members have answered "yes" to my question. They will compulsively want to know what's on that screen. And plenty will try to get a good gander. I once read an entire marketing strategy through the gap in the seats on Virgin East Coast.

I use the question to make a point about personal responsibility for security. As talented IT people, my team will tend to be great at making sure someone is getting all the technological security ducks in a row. We have people quantifying our Hacktivist risk and the threat from foreign intelligence agencies. We have password revision protocols, intrusion detection programmes and security incident management plans. We even go round confidently assuring the CEO that WannaCry can't possibly happen here. And yet we might just leave the strategic plan for all the world to see in Starbucks...

The point I'm making with this epic tale is that, in IT, we need to look past processes and tools to *behaviour*. As a discipline, I believe we have habitually given more attention to things than people, allowing people to behave as they prefer as long as the processes and tools are conforming.

Within a major digital change programme, it will not be possible for the team to behave as their personal preferences dictate. Just as they are responsible for security, they are also responsible for really scary stuff, such as communicating clearly, persuading, selling the dream, always keeping a cool head and toe-ing the party line on every issue when speaking with the business. Gulp!

And you will need to be a perfect role-model of these types of behaviour, every minute of every day. Bigger gulp!

So how can that be done?

Minimum skillset

Old dogs are actually very good at learning new tricks. They can sometimes be crafty enough not to want to bother.

You may very possibly need a programme of *education* as well as training. Your IT people may need to be educated and persuaded that doing things differently will be in their own self-interest. Hire a beyond-excellent communication and behaviour trainer or coach, who will begin by creating in the team an appetite for changing their ways. This has to be a person who can get them all to believe that if they make the effort to try the new approaches, their lives will be easier, with less resistance and quicker acceptance of their suggestions. This person will get the team to believe they can be trusted and valued for their skills and expertise if they behave a little differently. This is not fairy dust: educators like this really exist!

The minimum skill set you're looking to develop in everyone in your team – and not just those in business-facing roles, by the way – is:

- How to communicate at a level which is understood by each individual reader or listener. This includes jargon-busting explanatory skills, as jargon is the last refuge of the IT charlatan. They need to be able to pitch their explanations for all levels of knowledge, interest and agendas. One size does not fit all.

- How to make regular references to what the Programme is seeking to achieve, and what the benefits of making uncomfortable changes will be for end-users. They need to do this in a way which is convincing and natural. And yes, this IS code for "selling"! IT people within the Programme must be its best ambassadors and as such have a huge role to play in the engagement piece.

- How to deal calmly and positively with reluctance and resistance, including excellent listening skills and the empathy to see the situation from the other person's perspective. Having this type of attention and imagination will make them better problem-solvers and persuaders. You may also need to teach patience here.

- How to match their pace to the Programme timeline. Coming from BAU, some team members may not always have had to work against a Programme plan. One-paced people, diligent perfectionists and the easily-distracted may need some time management refreshment if they are to keep in step.

- How to stay on-message at all times, even when they themselves voted for an alternative solution to the one they are being asked to implement. They need the skills for toe-ing the line in a way which means they do not feel their integrity has been compromised. If this doesn't happen, the entire Programme is undermined by the Programme "owners" apparently disapproving of the Programme's content ... to people who will be all too ready to listen.

- How to work collaboratively within and beyond the team. I made the point at the start of Chapter 10 on hiring people, that collaborative team-working is the only way you'll make a complete success of a transformation Programme. It's certainly the only way to get it out of the door on time. So if your incumbent team has baggage, or a tendency to lone-wolfery, it needs to be persuaded to behave differently.

NB: building rafts in deepest Argyll in February is one type of team-building training. That definitely isn't what you need here. Instead, people need the skills for being open-minded to colleagues' ideas. They need techniques for communicating openly and calmly at all times. They need to be able to lose the battle to win the war.

Oh, and finally, just to reiterate that point you being the role model for all this... I am still working on 100% compliance myself.

There's nothing special about change

Having said all that, I wondered if there was anything unique about running a change team that's different to running, say, an Ops or IT team. I decided that, no, there isn't. The principles are the same for any team where the people are collegiate and bright.

My main rule is that there is no benefit in lengthy and forensic examination of failure. Self-motivated people will never repeat their mistakes and will not be spurred on by being beaten up. So when something goes wrong, learn from the mistake – and move on. Nothing to see here.

In Case of Emergency, Break Glass

Losing the Team

When the going gets tough, the tough get their CVs out. It happens quite regularly on most pressured transformations. What's the one best remedy for re-motivating and retaining disgruntled team members?

Dead simple. Listen to them.

As Transformation Lead, one of your key responsibilities is to make time for people - and make enough time to listen to them well and empathetically. That's everything from making time to hear about their weekend; to listening to their career aspirations; to letting them sound-off when it's not going well.

Listen in order to understand where the person is coming from. Don't assume you just need to nod and agree while they get it off their chest. Take whatever action you can to bring them back alongside. Often, showing you really *do* understand how tough they are having it can be enough.

If people are paid positive attention – both when they *do* and *don't* need it, you will stand a far better chance of retaining talent. In return, they will give you early-warning signals that they need attention, so you can address dissatisfaction before the place becomes Leaving Party Central.

15. Avoiding Mission Creep, Crumble and Crop

Keeping going

Once the Programme is running, it has to keep running. Common sense. But back in the real world, that's a challenging thing to do. Unexpected problems will appear; agendas and personalities will get in the way; and everyone's energy will have off-days. There are two main considerations for the "keeping going" phase:

a)   to have a project plan that keeps you to time; and

b)   to always be alert to the siren-call of changes and compromises that tempt you to sub-optimal delivery.

The challenges are Mission Creep, Crumble and Crop:

Mission Creep

To reduce your anxiety about mission creep, the first rule is: accept it. Creep is almost inevitable, because organisations and their environments change during the course of every transformation. The best you can do with mission creep is to accept it will happen; be aware that it has started to happen; and then control it.

If your Discovery exercise is thorough; your purpose statement is clear; and you have a good understanding of the business at the start, then it cannot wander too far.

You will need to be clear about your Triangle of Truth. Every programme has an anchor point on the Triangle of Truth which comprises:

Cost

Quality   Time

You will need to identify your anchor point on the triangle at the start – which of these three is non-negotiable for your Programme? Being clear about that will allow you to permit teensy bits of creep on the other two. So if the deadline is the deadline, then cost and quality could be allowed a little elasticity.

It is very useful to have this concept to hand when pressure is put on you by stakeholders. Explain the aim is to balance all three, but that Some Corners Are More Equal Than Others. It is a particularly effective tool when Nice-To-Have and Kids-In-A-Sweetshop Syndromes kick in.

But as I said, creep will inevitably occur. Sometimes there may be "positive creep" – when you need to accept that new circumstances have arisen and it's essential to accommodate these. As long as the business is happy to do so; you can deliver to an acceptable quality standard; the necessary funding is available; and time has been allowed, then no worries, mate.

Mission Creep can also occur when you've missed something in the early (Discovery) stages. Again, this is necessary creep. Admit the mistake, accommodate the new information and crack on.

Once you've recalibrated to take account of this new information – maybe even resetting your anchor-point on the Triangle - then you will need to communicate that to key stakeholders. From there onwards, be dogmatic about what we are here to do and how. Keeping your purpose statement and agenda visible will help keep people on the straight and narrow.

Mission Crumble: when it all goes to pieces

I'd say that Mission Crumble occurs when items from two or more Chapter subjects in this book go astray simultaneously. So you're not crumbling if your only problems are with suppliers delivering erratically – you simply have supplier challenges to address. Don't panic, Captain Mainwaring!

However, if you have supplier issues; and your in-house team is becoming dysfunctional; and/or your Executive Sponsor has glazed over; and/or an Alternative Transformation Programme is gaining traction in Finance, then yes, you're in the custard.

In this situation, good governance is your friend. Monitoring what's happening (or stalling) in the project at very regular governance meetings will alert you to parts of the Programme that might be fraying at the edges. And it should alert you well before things are so bad as to be irreparable. As Programme Lead, you should turn your attention very quickly to the wobbly areas, put them in Special Measures and it's likely they'll be retrieved.

Mission Crop: when business transformation becomes IT upgrade

We all start out with good intentions and an ambitious vision – to transform the organisation with IT at the heart of that transformation.

But such well-laid plans are very susceptible to mission creep. It's all too easy for people to lose sight of the vision when faced with the scale of the transformation task and non-negotiable deadlines. It's easy to tip into the world of mission crop, where big ambitions are not realised and return on the investment is not truly achieved. So how do you stop mission minimisation? My suggestions are:

Inspire the business

Truth is, most people in most organisations don't really want to change. Change requires hard work and risk. So culturally, most organisations will find every opportunity to stay exactly the same. If the business is not inspired by the possibilities that come with the proposed change, it will seek comfort-zone solutions – methods and mechanics that keep its world just about the same as it always was. No horizons will be widened.

So everyone in the business first needs to be inspired by the benefits and possibilities that the change will bring. That's not just the role of the CEO, sponsor or the Programme Lead. Everyone in IT can play a part in enthusing colleagues about the opportunities ahead. The Transformation Lead needs to inspire her team to be inspiring.

Unless you have buy-in from the business, and everyone in it being willing to run with the new technology to improve the business and innovate further, you will simply have refreshed the IT.

Be a disruptor

In IT, we've spent a long time in that windowless office on the eighth floor. We're used to waiting to be asked to get involved, usually to facilitate or implement other people's ideas for innovation. Maybe we're still not really used to exploiting our potential for taking a leadership role in the business. This can sometimes make us a little too passive. And so when colleagues press for familiar-as-possible solutions, we don't yet have the habit of challenging them.

Making that challenge will be uncomfortable - for everyone involved. Organisations can be perfectly fine with *change itself* being uncomfortable: indeed, "disruption" has changed from a negative to a positive concept in the last few years in most corporate lexicons. However, they can be less accepting of an IT team and its leader becoming disruptive. For four decades, IT have been compliant facilitators of the organisation's wishes. IT bursting out of the cupboard under the stairs like Vin Diesel may come as something of a shock.

But if the transformation programme is to succeed in full, IT will have to speak up, be persuasive and put its collective foot down. That means being recognised for your leadership and not easily pushed back into that cupboard.

My best tip here is for Transformation Leads is to use some communications coaching before the programme begins. It's extremely difficult to regain your voice *after* you've been drowned out, so coaching helps you speak out loudly and convincingly from the start.

Do what's right: not what's easy

During the build, everyone in IT is of course under enormous pressure. Deadlines are pressing and not negotiable and there is always far more to do than we anticipated at the start. It therefore becomes very tempting to use quick and easy solutions. Expedient shortcuts can result in all kinds of long-term disappointments, from reduced functionality and lost opportunities to lack of metrics and restrictions on further innovation.

I would recommend that the litmus test for solutions that save development time is just one question: "It's easy: but is it right?" If the solution fulfils the aims of the Programme, then it's perfect. But if it's expedient but doesn't deliver the programme's potential – then it's a false (time) economy and it's never right. It's just an upgrade. Your aim here is to stop your role in project leadership – i.e. delivering the vision – becoming project management, which is simply delivering a solution.

Do NOT plan to fix it later

Again, those looming deadlines are the enemy of fully achieving our vision. We all know how the argument goes: we know we *meant* to have that feature ready for go-live but it's proved tricky. So we agree to launch without it and retrofit it later. The IT will be upgraded at launch, but only part-way to what could have been.

In my experience, in reality people rarely go back and fix it later. They are overtaken by events. Other snags arise and take up time – or even other opportunities arise and catch our magpie-eyes. Users quickly get used to the upgrade – after all, it's better than what went before – and don't demand the solution they might have had.

I think the only way of avoiding delayed functionality – and therefore a sub-optimal solution at launch – is to identify in the project plan which features are absolutely non-negotiable if we are to meet the business objectives of the programme. These are therefore always priority developments and must always be fully functional at launch – the minimal viable product.

Challenge collective self-deception

Finally, the greatest enemy of achieving the full ambition of the programme is a very interesting psychological one. It usually manifests when someone in the C-suite suggests that they are beginning to sense that this organisation is *not quite ready for* such a profound change as the one we've been proposing. When this happens, it is often met with a chorus of approval. Frankly, I think that's because it lets everyone else off the hook – there'll be no need for the discomfort of change or risk if the transformation can be labelled as not quite right for the business at the moment. The comforting arms of business-as-usual beckon.

This collective self-deception is based on the worrying assumption that this transformation is about **THIS** organisation. But it almost never is. It's bigger than just us. Transformation is almost always necessary because of this organisation's *place in its market*. So if anyone else in your market or area of operation is already implementing the content of your transformation, your organisation needs to do it too. And quickly.

You will always need to challenge the introspection of "are we really ready for this?" with "We have no choice".

By this point, we've come full circle - Mission Crop in the C-suite occurs when there's been a failure of vision and/or engagement. You simply go back to the beginning of this list and re-engage...

In Case of Emergency, Break Glass

Creeped Out

Mission Creep is almost inevitable, because transformations are carried out in real time, and the real world changes every day. Crop and Crumble are also commonplace. It can be easy to stress about them: and even feel it has all been for nothing or you've full-on failed. No: it's just that life happened.

Your resilience can be improved by remembering you are looking for "the serenity to accept the things I cannot change; the courage to change the things I can; and the wisdom to know the difference."

The only further step after reminding yourself of that is pragmatic onward soldiering. Roll up your mental sleeves; read your purpose statement and your MVP; and move on.

16. When a wheel comes off

Getting over setbacks

Wheels will come off. With a bit of luck, they won't all come off at once. And all you'll need is a wheel brace, a spare tyre – or at very worst, the AA. Living in expectation of a problem arising will help. By expecting a problem, you're likely to spot the warning signs. But equally, you're less likely to panic, lose heart or feel you have to go and get another job. Transformation success is all about pragmatic resilience.

Early stage setbacks

Goal disallowed: what to do when the Board says no

You can't win 'em all, as we occasionally have to say at St James' Park, NE1. And in my experience of IT transformation, sometimes, despite your best efforts, three months of preparation and 874 brainy ideas, you take your proposed programme to the Board: and you get a resounding "no".

So what do you do then?

First up, just as in football, you do not punch the ref or mutter that the other team smells. Of course you are disappointed and possibly even furious, but when you hear that resounding no, you need to make every effort to park your emotions and really listen hard to the reasons given for rejecting your proposal. The Board will give you a few minutes grace to ask two or three questions to help you clarify where their objections lay – so pick the ones that will give you the best understanding of the root cause of their decision. Just keep it to a couple of questions, though – a long series of queries all beginning "Yes, but…" will make you look irritatingly defensive. Then leave, politely thanking them for their time.

Next, feel free to go and stand round the back of the office and kick the bins, providing no-one can see you. Once you've got a grip on your language, you're ready to go and tell your team.

Of course, they're going to be disbelieving, disappointed, disheartened, disapproving and disgusted. Possibly in that order. You'll need to let all those emotions be expressed. And once the grumbling has been given airtime, you'll be ready to start on the fixing stage.

First step in the fixing stage for me is to work out where we went wrong. You'll have your notes on what the Board said, which might include:

- **The figures**. Did we get it right, mathematically? Did we over-egg the content and so put the price up? Did we miss a bit, making us look like we were not being fully honest about costs? Did we fail to manage their expectations of what this programme might cost?

- **The angle**. Did we offer to fix the correct problem – i.e. had we got the problem statement right? Did we have a big enough solution? Or where we fixing things that weren't yet broken? Did we have the right amount of emphasis on each part of the solution we offered, or was there a wonky imbalance?

- **The timing**. Should we be fixing this now? Were we offering a solution that was too slow for the Board's agenda? Or scarily fast for the size/mood of this organisation? Might we even have presented at the wrong time of the financial year?

- **The communication**. Did we get our story right? Did we make the proposal clear – i.e. did they truly understand what we were trying to say and do? Did they get why the organisation needs to do this thing? Did we ensure they were worried enough about the consequences of *not* doing it?

- **The Other Things**. We don't know what we don't know – and the Board is not able to tell us what that is. What if there's a merger or acquisition imminent? Or a restructure? What if there are big budget cuts coming?

The questions will give you an insight into where it went wrong. They'll direct you towards the additional evidence, ideas or information you'll need to work on. However, they will only work if you answer them 100% honestly. Be prepared to admit – to yourself and to others – that you made an omission or a misjudgement.

Your answers will give you and the team an action plan. And you can divert the energy that you'd all planned to put into the programme to creating the revised proposal, with no tears before bedtime.

Don't rush it; do a really thorough job on the re-worked offer, because it has to be even more convincing now you've had a refusal. And while you're doing that, any Other Things That They Couldn't Tell You might see the light of day. So, chin up, ball on the centre spot, kick towards the goal...

Later stage setbacks

It's all in the mind

The Transformation Lead needs positive resilience; and the ability to front-up to disasters and setbacks. Kipling and all that (Rudyard, I mean: I'm not advising getting a lot of cakes in).

You will need to develop a three-way personality split: the ability to move between three different leadership styles. These are:

- the relationship manager

- a bit of command-and-control

- the trendy Richard Branson-ish one that devolves decision-making and accountability.

You'll need to don the right personality for the task in hand throughout the programme – and especially when something goes wrong.

Here's a worked example:

- Your Programme has hit the wall: everything you thought was going to work … just doesn't.

- Assume your relationship-manager personality. This is what you'll need to use with the project sponsor, usually the Board and/or the senior management team. It's a tricky one to get right because, in a crisis, the sponsor needs to be told at once that there *is* a crisis. And that sponsor sure ain't gonna like it. So in relationship-manager mode, it's your job to make sure the sponsor first really understands the problem. What precisely is wrong, and what are the implications of that? Then, once everyone has stopped running around the room screaming, you need to make sure the senior team members all believe that the problem can be solved. As the shouting stops, and the emotional temperature begins to steady, you then need to get their permission to solve the problem; and to give reassurance that this can be made to happen. That's quite a journey to take people on: only relationship-managing gets a result with the sponsor, I've found.

- Next, on the walk back down the stairs from the top floor to the Transformation Team office, you'll need to morph into command-and-control mode. This *does not* mean you need to take a deep breath, ready to start shouting. It means you need to accept and own the problem. And *want* to direct the solution. And develop a coherent plan to fix it.

I believe that a crisis is not a problem that you should swiftly and neatly give away to a giant multinational provider, assuring everyone that it's best if the Big Boys come in with all their bells and whistles. For me, you need to keep ownership in-house, with the solution being developed where you can keep an eye on it, under your control. That said, this is not a time to save a few quid, either.

If your crisis is large, you need to throw your best resources at it. That means hand-picking the most able, innovative and collaborative team you can get your paws on (and by the way, that usually includes the best lawyers). And you'll need decent capacity levels, too.

- Once you've got the team lined up, swap back into relationship-manager gear. Your role is now to make this team believe the problem can be solved; and that they can solve it. You'll need to create a positive atmosphere; you know, the one which has been slipping away from the team in the last few weeks of increasing gloom or frustration. You need them enthusiastic and energised if you want them to be creative and innovative. These people need to know that they can do the impossible. By next Tuesday.

- Then, you will then need a final quick-change into a third type of leader: the trendy modern empowerer. Yes, sure, you OWN the problem, but David Brent-style my-way-or-the-highway is no way to get the best out of talented team members. So tell everyone they can make any decisions that fit with their remit and their recognised skill and judgement. Encourage solutions that don't follow well-trodden paths, if these will fix the job. And give credit for those lightbulb ideas that really move the project on. The team members will all then do their bit to solve the problem for you...

Running to catch up

The most likely wheel to come off is the one relating to time. Because Transformation occurs in the real world, there are a zillion reasons why there may be delays, from broken legs to global pandemics. As with Mission Creep, accept that it is likely that you will become short of time. My top tips for this situation are:

- **The MVP route.** From the very start of the programme, always keep a clear view of your minimum viable product. What's the absolute basic content you will need to launch by the date? Knowing what your must-haves and must-wins are will keep it all in perspective. Focusing on getting this content ready by the deadline will ensure the greatest percentage of success.

- **Fess up.** Don't be afraid to say that you're running out of time. As I've said time and again, fear of failure, appearance-maintenance and sweeping things under the carpet won't help. Don't hide the problems, but lay them bare and discuss them with the relevant stakeholders.

- **You need your champion**. Ask for support from your Programme sponsor. You will need that person's help in persuading those at the top of the organisation that the situation is still positive.

- **Right size it.** Meet with stakeholders to agree a right-sized version of the launch. Agree whether it with be later, slighter or dearer, in accordance with the Triangle of Truth (Chapter 15, *Mission Creep*).

- **Be ruthless.** If right-sizing means cuts to quality or budget, then be bold and ruthless and do what it takes. Half of everything will please no-one, so you may need to limit your disappointed audience to certain areas/departments. Be forensic with your cuts. Your judgement here is always based on minimising negative impact on customers.

- **Accept it**. If you have mission crop, then hey, you have mission crop. At least you have gone live some degree of transformation. Things are better than before.

Broke Glass, Pulled Lever, Nothing Happened

So what's the emergency fix for a chapter about emergency fixes? What do you do when your final solution doesn't work and you're all out of ideas?

You phone a friend.

Digital transformation usually occurs in pressured situations and no-one is immune to the strain. Consequently, I would strongly advise getting yourself a coach before you begin the Programme. A skilled executive coach will be there for the good days as well as the bad, being a sounding board for your strategic or development ideas; or helping you clarify where you can take your skills next. For the most part, coaching is about positive development – mine calls it "making good people excellent". But equally, a coach will be there on the chucking-in-the-towel and can't-think-straight days, helping you clarify your thoughts and taking the emotion out of any hasty decision making you might later regret.

If you're lucky, you'll also have a mentor you can call when it all turns to dust. A coach might not be from your professional discipline, but rather a specialist in clear thinking; whereas a mentor will be someone who *is* an expert in your world and has done it all before. Experienced expertise may very well get you back on the road to recovery. Who have you previously worked for or with, whose judgement you respect? Would that person give you half an hour of their time on the phone?

Whether you choose one of these or both, you're doing the right thing by asking for help. There's no shame in not knowing what to do: and there's strength in recognising when you need a bit of help.

17.The Big Finish

Ending the programme

When it comes to ending the programme, it's the little things that matter. As you transition from development to support, you are highly likely to be focused on the big stuff that needs to be tweaked/fixed/polished/delivered. But you'll also need to keep an eye out for the twiddly bits on your clipboard with the Monumental Checklist of Things We Mustn't Forget. It's usually the little bits that make all the difference.

What are they, then? For me, there are six strands of activity you need to think about for transition. And within those, there are few easy-to-forget things that it's essential to remember….

1. Don't skimp on the communication

Everybody involved now needs to hear one more time the current position/destination/route/steps/ timing/etc, etc, etc. Interestingly, the communications piece here is often more straightforward than it has been at many previous stages - finally, after all these years, you're seeing concrete reality approaching. Hallelujah – cue flags, bunting and a modestly-sized brass band. So go for your life with your Directorial Briefing Packs, customer interface seminars, staff countdown newsletters… whatever you think needs communicating.

But don't forget the points-to-note reminders – which are very often about process change. For example, Eric will have been told that the report he usually runs on a Monday will now be out on a Tuesday and in a different format. But it's wise to remind him and prepare him for the change now, a little way out, so that it is expected and more-normaller when it comes.

2. This is not just engagement; it's *active* engagement

Yes, you've told everyone everything they need to know. At least twice. But for years, your project has been conceptual and a-long-way-in-the-future. Now it's coming to life.

So the next consideration is to check everyone who matters – and that might be almost everyone involved – is *actively* engaged with this project. You need everyone switching on their full wattage to share knowledge and believe this now involves them. So for example:

BAU needs to be involved super-early, months before the go-live. Their processes work well now and they'll have been involved in designing the new processes, but let's get them thinking about *all* the ramifications of the new processes. They'll spot problems, but they'll also have ideas and solutions, ensuring accidents don't happen.

Or take training. Of course you've thought of training. But here's an idea - what might be done now to make all system users responsible for their own learning about the new system, so that they are, er, *obliged* to be actively engaged?

3. The dress rehearsal

Of course you'll be chewing your way through ITIL – the giant ITIL manual on transition is taken as read. Implementing the prescribed steps and checks will avert most disasters.

But there's always something that any amount of checks cannot avoid. So it's cue spotlights: full dress rehearsal time. You'll need costumes, props, and everyone knowing their lines. You need to involve key stakeholders, power-users and all the kit. You need the run-through to check what's (not) working, what's (not) connecting, and what's fallen through the gap in the floorboards and cannot be prised out even with the breadknife and a bent coathanger.

Alongside that is remembering to check that there are the right resources in place to be able to cope, e.g. in BAU. Or whether in fact you need sign-off on more resources, followed by high-speed hiring and up-to-speeding. And er, who's going to do that?

And you'll also need to remember to tell everyone what we've got in the cupboard – what's the service catalogue of all the offerings within the new system? And what's the knowledge-base – how will system users find out the answers to their questions? Who can help them with what types of queries?

4. Prepare for problems

I think it's easy to avoid preparing for a problem. We don't *forget* about this, but we Transformers don't *like* telling the sponsor/client that something might go wrong – it tends to make people a touch antsy. We also like to believe we've thought of everything (we write long lists on clipboards, you know, to be sure). But in fact, back in the real world, however much thought and innovation and testing and care we've used, the system ain't going to be Grade AAA+ Class 1 perfect when it launches. With a lot of care and a bit of luck, any problems will have the status of snags and hiccups. But even these are still A Problem.

If A Problem happens, you're aiming to score zero on the Headless Chicken Scale. You'll need to be instantly prepared so that you know whose problem it is; and what they're going to do about it.

That means you need to remember to create and discuss a Problem Escalation Protocol, which states at precisely what level the issue is the responsibility of the CIO; the Programme Sponsor; the Board and the CEO. Think of "discussing discomfort" as an essential part of your communication campaign and it might be a bit easier to talk about it...

5. Perfection is a work in progress

Despite all the above anticipatory thinking, you're going to need a second edition of the new system far sooner than you'd planned. It'll become clear on Day 2 that some stuff isn't quite perfect. In fact, you probably *already* know some of the stuff that's going into the Second Edition before launch.

Therefore, before you launch, you're going to need a plan to fix all the stuff that wasn't quite 100% by the time you went live. With space in it for the stuff you then found out didn't meet the users' expectations. Which means you need a plan for the second release date, even before you start.... Oh, and that means you're straight back in development, and needing another delivery plan, too. Launch is the end of the first journey and the start of the second journey. Don't forget to put that in big letters in your communications' campaign.

Carry lessons over for the next time. Especially in multi-point/stage transformations, you will need constant objective assessments of lessons learned at every stage. In the relief of getting the ruddy thing out of the door, don't forget to learn, review and change it for next for time. Once again, there's no shame in not being perfect the first time – but shame on you if you make the same mistake twice.

6. It's the little things...

And finally: don't forget the printers – or whatever peripheral matter it is that you've probably forgotten, because smart people forget simple things. You need to check your fangle-dangle new system is configured so it speaks to the printers, or fits on the desks, or recognises the passwords, or isn't scheduled to launch on Easter Monday.

The best way to do this is to ask a nice realistic person who has had nothing to do with the project to give you some suggestions of where their capable-but-IT-amateur eye thinks it might go wrong. They'll be far more likely to spot the schoolboy error than you will from your ivory tower on the eighth floor.

In Case of Emergency, Break Glass

All good things come to an end

For many people in IT, a major transformation can be a roller coaster, but an exhilarating ride. So it can sometimes be difficult to admit that it's over. This is especially true if leading the transformation has brought you recognition and respect; or you've enjoyed the adrenalin buzz of having something exciting to do which shows really tangible results.

When the natural lifespan of the transformation ends, it can be quite difficult to acknowledge that it's over, and you're back to – yawn! - the old days of BAU. It can be tempting to keep the party going, changing things that don't need it or continuing the spending spree. However, overdoing it will very quickly erode any reputational gains you have made with your achievements.

So you need to recognise when it's time to stop. And if life looks very dull after that, it may be time to hand BAU to someone who enjoys it and go and ride another rollercoaster.

You're gonna have to face it, you're addicted to change.

18. The Agile Mindset

Transformation skills for the future

To conclude then: if all this is what transformation needs now, how can we be sure it'll be what you need when you get to the end of your programme? After all, it could take you several years to complete – mine usually do.

I'm not starting some De-Lorean-inspired time travelling debate. Nor is it crystal-ball Mystic Meggery. I am making the point that we are working within a very rapidly changing environment. In the 2020s we face the long tail of a pandemic; recovery from a sharp global recession; increasingly cagey worldwide trading relationships; above-board and underhand applications of vast datasets; criminal state and commercial security attacks; and technological innovation exploding in all directions.

In this environment, the successful Transformation Lead is going to need the skills and brass-neck confidence to quickly read the runes; think creatively every time; and take rapid action. You will need an agile mindset. That's nothing to do with a preference for agile development; but an ability to jump quickly into all kinds of New Normals.

I would define the agile mindset that Transformation Leads need as one that has no fear of innovation – even on a large scale, with risk and/or at high speed. It is a mindset confident to make changes because the basis for the change is rooted in intelligent analysis and well-considered weighing of alternative solutions. And the agile mindset means the Lead is able to take decisions on innovation quickly because she has had her eye on the wider horizon in the preceding months and years. She saw this coming.

Eyes on the prize: and eyes on the horizon.

Mark Aikman is an internationally-recognised technology leader. He specialises in delivering IT/digital and business transformation, usually in complex, worldwide and high-risk environments.

He lives in Kent with his family and some high-maintenance chickens.

www.ignitiontransformation.co.uk

Printed in Great Britain
by Amazon